Excerpts from the 1971 Journal of Rosemary Mayer

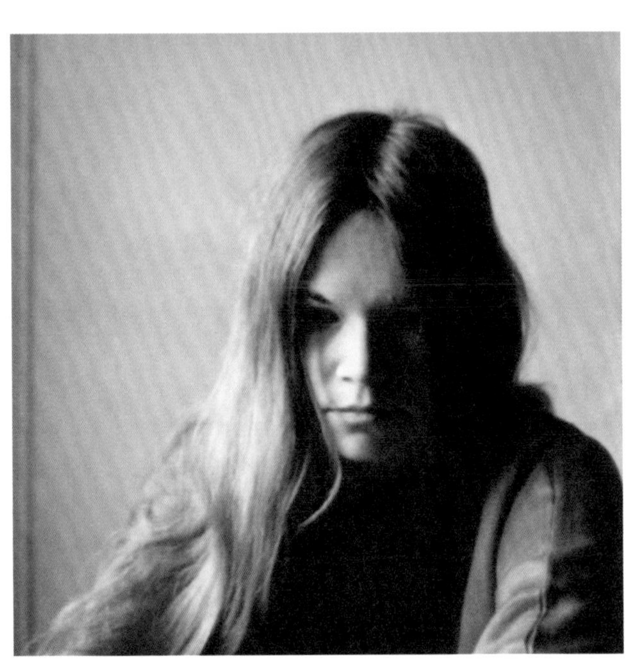

Excerpts from the 1971 Journal of Rosemary Mayer

Edited by Marie Warsh

Soberscove Press
Chicago

Soberscove Press
Chicago, Illinois
soberscove.com

First published by Object Relations in 2016 on the occasion of the exhibition, "Rosemary Mayer: Conceptual Works and Early Fabric Sculptures, 1969–1973," at SOUTHFIRST Gallery, Brooklyn, NY. Copyediting & Proofreading: Susan Bee. Design: Almog Cohen-Kashi

All materials courtesy of the Estate of Rosemary Mayer

ISBN 978-1-940190-25-9
Library of Congress Control Number: 2019953103
Mayer, Rosemary (1943–2014)
Excerpts from the 1971 Journal of Rosemary Mayer / edited by Marie Warsh

Design: Hour Studio
Copyediting & Proofreading: Anna Vitale
Printed in the United States of America

Distributed by
ARTBOOK | D.A.P.
75 Broad Street, Suite 630
New York, NY 10004
artbook.com

Frontispiece: Photograph of Rosemary Mayer, c. 1971. Pages 45–49: Photographs of *Veils* by Rosemary Mayer. Pages 23, 33, 58, 69, 99, 108, 138, 149: Photographs taken by Rosemary Mayer of her apartment at 383 Broome Street, c. 1970. Vito Acconci and John Campione appear in the photographs on pages 58 and 99, respectively.

Cover: Rosemary Mayer, *Veils II*, 1971. Burlap and nylon. 10 ft × 6 ft.

Contents

Editor's Introduction (2020)

Preparing this introduction to the expanded edition of *Excerpts from the 1971 Journal of Rosemary Mayer* has been a process of reflection. A lot has happened in the three years since the first edition was published: additional shows and publications of Rosemary's work, new research by scholars, and a website. In some instances, it was the journal that led directly to new projects. Julia Klein, publisher of Soberscove Press, read and loved the journal and subsequently sought out the estate with the idea for a publication about Rosemary's work. This resulted in *Temporary Monuments: Work by Rosemary Mayer,* 1977–1982. Published in 2018, the book consists of documentation of Rosemary's ephemeral installations and sculptures, and it is the first presentation of this body of work. This project led us back to the journal, when Julia suggested that Soberscove publish a second edition. In addition to making the publication more widely available, this project also offered the opportunity to share more of Rosemary's writing about her life in 1971. The goal to reveal more, I am now realizing, made this project feel very different than when I was working on the first edition.

When I compiled the first edition, exactly three years ago, Rosemary was relatively unknown as an artist. The project was conceived as part of her first major show since the 1980s as a way to provide an introduction to Rosemary and a context for her work—

and to give her a voice. Between the pages of her journal, I found a curious document that spoke to her own desire and struggle for visibility as an artist—a handwritten letter from 1970 by Sol LeWitt, addressed to the Museum of Modern Art, that declared "Rosemary Mayer is a real artist." I like to imagine the scenario in which this letter was conceived—perhaps at a dinner party at which Rosemary expressed frustration about the lack of interest in her work, leading LeWitt, known for his generosity with other artists, to offer this endorsement. Small holes at the top of the document suggest that it was tacked to the wall, perhaps in her studio, a reminder for someone whose confidence in herself often wavered. Reflecting on the editing process for the first edition of *Excerpts from the 1971 Journal of Rosemary Mayer,* I realize now that my intent was to show that Rosemary was indeed a real artist.

At first I was apprehensive about introducing her through her journal. It felt like a great responsibility, overwhelming at times, to have access to this material and to figure out how to present it. While I wanted to portray her honestly, I also wanted to respect her privacy. In a journal from the late 1970s, she wondered about who would eventually read her journals, but she was not writing for an audience. While working on this project, my perspectives kept shifting—from niece, to art historian, to co-manager of Rosemary's estate—in a way that was somewhat confusing. I worried that her incessant expressions of self-doubt would turn people off. I decided to keep it short.

But Rosemary's struggles, which I was worried about sharing, were what readers responded to most. Many artists and women, and particularly women artists, expressed feeling like they could really relate to Rosemary's artistic development and were struck by her honesty and self-awareness. Art historian Katie Geha, who curated a show of Rosemary's work at the University of Georgia, Athens, was impressed by the convergence of art and daily life that defined Rosemary's world. Geha wrote to me: "I find comfort in the

Feb. 8, 1970

Dear Museum of Modern Art,

Rosemary Mayer is a real artist.

Sol LeWitt

familiarity of her writing; that making the rent to inventing new ways to drape fabric to finding a connection with a friend or a lover exist on a continuum, one that refuses to remain fixed." From this and other comments, I became interested in how Rosemary's journal could seem so personal and rooted in a particular time and place, but also be so transcendent and accessible.

My approach to editing the expanded edition of the journal was informed by feedback from readers as well as having developed a better understanding of Rosemary's purpose for her journal. In 1971, Rosemary read *The Diary of Anaïs Nin*, which made a big impression on her. She criticizes Nin for being "too good," for not including sex, food, and weather—the stuff of daily life with which Rosemary was so preoccupied. Rosemary explains in her journal that, in contrast to Nin, she was trying "to include everything that's happening to me." Because this was important to Rosemary, I wanted to provide more of a sense of this "everything." With more than double the material of the first edition, this new edition is less fragmentary, reading more as a narrative. I have, however, still edited out a lot in order to respect what I imagine she would have wanted to keep private.

My approach was also informed by my own interests and personal connection to Rosemary. I was particularly fascinated with her documentation of and commentary on all the books she was reading, the art she was seeing, and the movies she was watching. All of this provided a window into Rosemary and her interests as well as both popular and art culture of the time. Her critiques and enthusiasms also felt so familiar—evidence of Rosemary's erudition and lifelong love of art, books, and movies, which she often shared with me and others. For this expanded edition, I included additional entries with these references and then compiled an appendix of all of the books and movies she recorded having read (or intended to read) and watched that year.

I believe the ambitiousness of her reading in this particular year also relates to her larger goal to "push boundaries," a phrase she uses several times. This boundary pushing applies not only to her desires for artistic development but also to her life. In 1971, she experiments with new approaches to draping, layering, and painting fabric. She experiments with drugs and tries yoga and fasting. She participates in a women's consciousness-raising group; she illegally collects unemployment benefits; she learns how to play chess. She describes reading Claude Lévi-Strauss and others as "HARD WORK," but she presses on. As Rosemary details in her journal, this was all the work of being an artist, and it was filled with challenges and obstacles, but also wonder and revelation. In an entry on March 10, she declares, "Art pushes the boundaries where afghans & scarves & pillowcases don't," but then asks, "Could they?" Indeed, it is apparent time and again in her journal how Rosemary was able to imbue the mundane with a sense of potential and power, a capacity that she maintained and continued to develop throughout her life and career.

Marie Warsh
Brooklyn, NY

Foreword (2016)

Rosemary Mayer's work speaks to a contemporary generation of artists working between mediums. Her pieces span language, drawing, painting, sculpture, and ephemeral performance. Marie Warsh has edited a portion of her aunt Rosemary's journals, which she inherited along with her brother and sister. Marie chose the year 1971 as a significant point in Mayer's development as an artist. 1971 happens to be the year art historian Linda Nochlin posed the question, "Why have there been no great woman artists?" in her famous essay of that title. This query could be said to frame Mayer's work of that year. Between her separation from her husband and her participation as a founding member of A.I.R. Gallery, in 1972, 1971 shows Mayer in the process of becoming an artist: attending feminist consciousness-raising groups, living alone, and starting to make rigorous work. Journal writing was a central part of Mayer's life. This publication represents just one year in a decades-long project to chronicle her experiences and also her thoughts and feelings. No portion of her journal has previously been published. It gives a glimpse not only into Mayer's work and her context (Adrian Piper, Hannah Weiner, A.I.R., SoHo in the early 1970s), but also might be resonant to any artist setting out to make work at any time—with all the fervor, ambition, doubts, insecurities, lassitudes, and lunges of discovery that process entails.

This publication comes as part of a series of exhibitions that I curated at SOUTHFIRST Gallery in Brooklyn on the theme of poetry and visual art. Starting in 2013, these included Robert Grenier's "Language Objects: Letters in Space, 1970–2013" (with Jay Sanders), "Susan Bee: Photograms and Altered Photos from the 1970s," which explored Bee's work in photography during the years in which she collaborated on the production of the experimental poetry magazine *L=A=N=G=U=A=G=E* (1978–1981), and "Rosemary Mayer: Conceptual Works & Early Fabric Sculptures, 1969–1973" (with Marie Warsh and Max Warsh), which begins with Mayer's process-based text works made in relation to the poetry magazine *0 TO 9*. Thanks to Florian Altenburg, Charles Bernstein, and Carol Greene/Greene Naftali Gallery for the continued vital feedback and support that has made these exhibitions possible. This publication would not be possible without the kind permission of the Estate of Rosemary Mayer. While transcribing, editing, and publishing the entire journal is beyond the scope of this exhibition series, it is our hope that this modest contribution is just the beginning of a larger editorial effort undertaken by a publisher to make Mayer's journal available in its entirety.

Maika Pollack
Founder and Director
SOUTHFIRST Gallery
Brooklyn, NY

Editor's Introduction (2016)

Often when I visited Rosemary during the 1990s, her journal would be on display. It was a large ledger with a hard, black cover trimmed in red. The pages were lined and the page numbers printed on the top corners. It was most often on a table, propped open on a dictionary stand, and this presentation made me wonder if she was not writing in this book but looking at it, reading it; a closer look confirmed that this was not her current journal but one written in the 1970s. I marveled at its size; it had a density that made it seem more like a novel. Pages and pages—exactly 300, I recently confirmed—of her disciplined cursive in various colors of ink. I wondered why it was on display: I was too young and my own journal practice too sporadic to imagine that reading one's journal from the past could be interesting or revelatory, and I couldn't understand how a diary could be a personal historical record.

The next time I saw the journal was in 2013 when I helped her move from her loft in Tribeca, where she had lived for forty years, to a small garden apartment in Park Slope, Brooklyn. In the corner of her vast loft was an old, battered black trunk filled with journals, including the one I had seen, other similar ledgers, and many other notebooks. In Park Slope, they were returned to the trunk, which became her coffee table, the centerpiece of her small living room. Knowing what was inside sometimes imbued the trunk with strange gravity.

Now the journals are in my living room in cardboard boxes. Over the past year, I've been drawn to reading them as a way of discovering a person with whom I was very close. But as I've delved into those from the 1960s and 1970s, I've begun to see their resonance beyond our connection because of the way she observed and recorded the world as well as the larger community of artists and poets with which she was involved.

Rosemary wrote that one of her intentions with her journal was to capture the "flavor" of her days. This excerpted and edited presentation of her record of 1971, taken from one of these large ledger journals, is also intended to provide a flavor of her experience as a woman and artist in downtown New York at this time. It is conceived as a compliment to the show, "Rosemary Mayer: Conceptual Works and Early Fabric Sculptures, 1969–1973," presented from October 2016 to January 2017 at SOUTHFIRST Gallery, and organized by myself, my brother Max Warsh, and Maika Pollack, curator and gallery director. The show includes a selection of Rosemary's early works, most of them on display for the first time since the period in which they were made. In addition to the journal writing, this volume includes images of some of the work she was making at this time (most of which no longer exists) and reproductions from a sketchbook.

I chose 1971 because it seemed in many ways a turning point for Rosemary. She was clearly interested in various ways of documenting her life and, in her archive, I discovered a series of life timelines that provide brief summaries for each year. In one, for 1971, she described herself as "Healthy thinking quiet solitary artist—artist just beginning—full of time." In another, she summarized the year: "I had dealers come to see my work. Art all the time. Lots of good friends. Incidental love affairs." She had been focused on being an artist since attending the Brooklyn Museum School from 1964–65, followed by the School of Visual Arts (SVA) from 1967–69. One of the first public presentations of her work was in *0 TO 9*, the journal of experimental art and writing edited by her sister, poet Bernadette Mayer, and Rosemary's husband, Vito Acconci, to whom she was married between 1962 and 1968. Her work from this period, some of which is included at SOUTHFIRST, shows her experimenting with conceptual art and writing. By 1971, she was breaking away from this framework and began working more seriously with fabric as a primary medium, creating sculptures and drawings that would lead to her first shows and a deepening involvement in the art world. Rosemary began working in fabric as an outgrowth of her painting practice, which in the late 1960s involved disassembling the stretched canvas and exploring the formal properties of canvas on its own. In 1971, she created a series of sculptures called *Veils*, which involved painting on, layering, and hanging various types of fabric. She regularly made drawings as part of both the process of making her sculptures and as individual works.

She was showing this work to friends and, as she noted, to dealers. She struggled to define it amidst the dominant currents of Minimalism, Conceptual Art, and Performance Art, and she contended with criticism from some friends and peers who said her work was too beautiful and object-oriented. She was sometimes overcome with self-doubt. However, she was also starting to become, as she declared somewhat triumphantly in early February, "one of those people who lives & breathes art."

In 1971, Rosemary was living on Broome Street in an apartment over the bakery for Café Roma, the long-standing café in the heart of Little Italy. (She once told me that that the apartment always smelled like pastry.) She had been there since 1966, having moved there with Acconci. After they split up in 1968, she lived there alone. Photographs Rosemary took of this space in 1970 are included in this volume.

By 1971, she and Acconci were on good terms, often

hanging out with his partner and collaborator, Kathy Dillon. Other close friends frequently mentioned in this year (often abbreviated in the journal with the initial of their first names) are Adrian Piper, whom she met at SVA and whose early 1970s *Catalysis* performances she documented in photographs for the artist; artist Donna Dennis, whom she met through a mutual connection to the poet Ted Berrigan; John Campione, a printer (who printed editions for Sol LeWitt, among other artists); poet Hannah Weiner; and Mary Hilgeman, a friend from St. Joseph's College in Brooklyn, which they both attended from 1960–62. Some of these relationships were informed by her regular participation in a consciousness-raising group, which became a popular form of feminist activism during the 1970s. The core members of the group consisted of Piper, Dennis, Grace Murphy (a friend from high school), Randa Haines (who became a filmmaker), and Jane Weiss. At times she seemed a little skeptical of these meetings, as she called them; yet they provided a valuable experience of camaraderie, raising issues about women's place in the world and in history. These experiences would influence future directions of her work. The show at SOUTHFIRST includes *The Catherines* (1972–73) and *Lady of the Mercians* (1973), part of a series of fabric sculptures inspired by the lives of historical women and the culmination of her work using fabric. In 1972, Rosemary became a founding member of A.I.R. Gallery, the first woman's cooperative gallery, and exhibited work from this series of sculptures there in 1973.

Although this journal is rooted in the New York art scene of the 1970s, aspects transcend it. Living and breathing art can make other forms of living and breathing a challenge, and Rosemary was often preoccupied with the exigencies of daily life, in particular with figuring out how to make money. After losing her job at a temp agency, she began collecting illegal unemployment and worked as a model for the painter Raphael Soyer. She spent considerable time thinking about things other than art, taking pleasure in food, friends, sex, cats, books, and movies. However, she also worried about being drawn away from art, about having enough time to work on her art. She has moments of being unmotivated and depressed. The question was how to make it all work and fit together into a fulfilling life. Sometimes she seems to figure it out. At the end of 1971, she embarks on a more serious romantic relationship, and a couple of months into it realizes, "Love & art & me aren't incompatible."

Rosemary abbreviated many words and names in her journal, likely as a way to write faster. For clarity, some of these abbreviations have been written out and the rest have been standardized. Some punctuation was added, and spelling errors were also fixed for clarity. For some entries she did not include a date, but it was possible to determine the date based on surrounding entries. These are included in brackets. All ellipses are Rosemary's.

Thank you to Donna Dennis, Farrar Fitzgerald, Maria McGarrity, Maika Pollack, Gillian Sneed, Max Warsh, Sophia Warsh, and Lewis Warsh for their assistance with this project.

Marie Warsh
Brooklyn, NY

Journal Excerpts

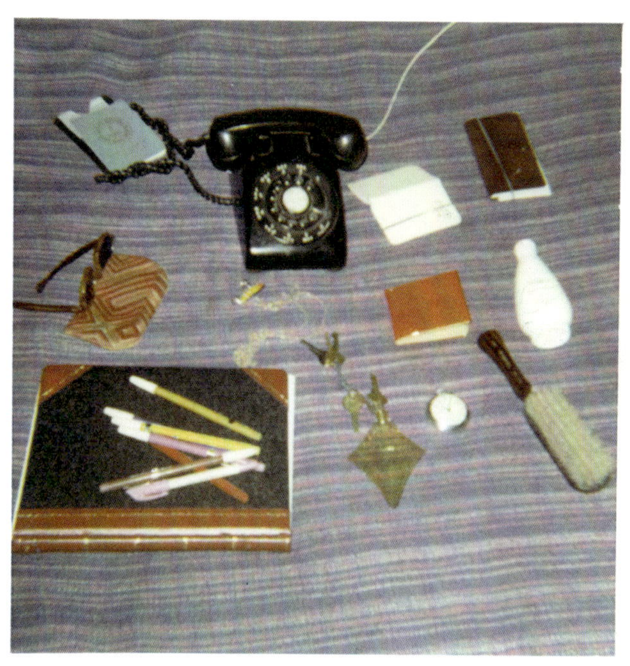

Friday Jan. 1, 1971 6:30PM

Yellow satin & white paint is an illusion (is that the right word) of light like blue one is of liquid.

Very funny state tonight. Restoned fr. last night w.o. new grass.—

New thoughts: to stop being invulnerable—before everything could get to me—now nothing can—the next step is to let selected aspects of the real stuff of days get to me. New Year's thought—

Since last Sat.: No work—emptied the walls, hung up about 6' square of dacron but nothing. I labeled another (duplicate) set of slides & I am all prepared to go up there on Tues. I really think I'll do it.

V & K may have found a loft.[1] They are too busy.

Sun. I went to Bay Ridge & saw Noberini.[2] Boring. Gossip.

Mon. nite John & I went to see Gimme Shelter.[3] Mick Jagger worship.

Wed. found out the drawing place isn't buying until after Jan. 15.

Another one in the Voice to check out on Thurs. Mon. Hannah is giving me some material.[4]

1 Artist Vito Acconci and his girlfriend Kathy Dillon. Rosemary and Vito married in 1962; they separated in 1968 but stayed friends for several years.

2 Mary Noberini, a classmate of Rosemary's from St. Joseph's College, which she attended from 1960–62.

3 Artist John Campione, a close friend and occasional lover.

4 The poet Hannah Weiner worked as a lingerie designer for A. H. Schreiber Co. and would often supply Rosemary with fabric. Rosemary calls her "H" throughout the journal.

The Aloneness hit me briefly this afternoon. To have continuity with no one.

Thurs. nite cooked dinner for John. Scallops & fennel & sweet potato. A good meal. But he was wrecked fr. being stoned. Too low keyed a New Year's Eve. John has a girlfriend, whose good points, he says, are "sweetness" and being flat-chested.

Thurs. January 7, 1971

It's freezing. Cookie cooking. Hazy-headed either fr. Thursday collapse or maybe it's too much V & K—Look what the cat's done. New cat—Leibinity—all those monads stretching in the morning sunshine.

Drying hair in Ridgewood backyard.[5] Pecan-Apple-Fennel Cookies—but they taste dull.

I took the slides to Bykert & Curtis says he will be there in Mar. to look. They are at Paula Cooper's now.[6] The Cultural Center is still up in the air.

I made a diagonal piece an almost square rectangle turned on the diagonal & I will make more rectangular pieces turned diagonally—w. string for folds & the paint—it looks so much like sails—bec. it's loose. Paint almost horizontal—a little off—I like it that way.

Things to think about—illusion—does it still happen w. o. a flat surface? It seems I've solved all the problems I set out to—getting my idiosyncratic choices out of there, taste and arrangement—making something that makes itself—letting things be themselves—finding a way that gives room to let colors play—the process makes the art—but now maybe it's fine to take this so far and go further—the diagonal rectangle—will allow the fabric to drape whc. I've

5 This may be a memory of growing up in Ridgewood in Brooklyn.

6 Rosemary was contacting some of the more prominent galleries at the time and inviting them to see her work. Bykert Gallery, located on the Upper East Side from 1966 until 1975, was one of the most influential. "Curtis" refers to the art dealer Klaus Kertess, the co-founder and director. In subsequent entries, Rosemary refers to him as "CC" or "KK" and again as "Curtis." Paula Cooper established the first gallery in Soho and, in 1971, was showing the work of Lynda Benglis, Robert Grosvenor, and Joel Shapiro.

always wanted to have happen but would never see my way to letting happen—there never seemed to be justification

With stain (long oblong shape) horizontal—they will look like water—definitely very liquid—& placid & natural as opposed to the very unplacid diagonal—whc. reminds me of sails and the string helps that connotation.

!Imagine that!----------------> A piece that's 2 pieces of fabric—2 dif. fabrics ---------------------

Macy's tom. for fabric

Have to think up some way of putting down a lot of close colors all next to one another—watercolors and gouache.

Narrow minded bastards who think objects are only decoration—automatically assuming that bec. a thing is attractive or interesting to look at it's not anything else. Real visual art has to continue—it's a human need—to see challenging beautiful things—& beauty is in the nature of materials as equally as it is in thoughts, process, structures, activities, reactions.

Beauty—Taste? Compare art & architecture—No one would want a Rauschenberg building—Robert Morris' stuff looks like buildings—old rect. bldg.

Paint drips, tin cans, rust, tires, old junk—pitted beams—that's a sensibility— the means & there's a message all that JJ shit about frontality & the plane & flatness & painterliness—paint flat stuff w. chiaroscuro strokes—the artist's elegant marks—

In Oldenberg's drawings too—elegant marks. Amazing Rothko & Newman are dead—there's an elegance—but not so personalized as to show the hand, the brush—but the way w. paint—

Things are down to the basics now w. me—no, they were with the canvas & orange paint pieces—they're going on now to new stuffs—new fabrics—the paint's still the same—more play w. colors now.

Wed. Jan. 20 11:00 AM

Thursday peace made cookies.

Friday piece which now looks too terrible.

Sat. brought grey paint. Pizza. Phillip until 1PM Sun.[7]

Tired all day Sun. Finally at 11:30 began work on red & blue tricot piece finished it at 3:30.

Mon. potato pancakes & applesauce for John. Feeling incoherent, cold, nervous.

Tuesday calls to CC & P Cooper. Dinner w. Linda. Talk w. Adrian.[8]

This AM Bob Stern fr. Paula Cooper. Unnerving—no opinion.

Linda's invited me to her house Sat. night. Adrian's convinced me I ought to go.

It's really cold. 10 degrees this AM—now at 11—for the third day.

The cats are all over. The little one is getting really lovely. He's almost pink.

Full of thoughts I need time to write down. About selling work. About not being in love w. Phillip. About ego.

Got to go to work.

7 Phillip was a friend and lover. Little is known about some of the friends Rosemary mentioned in the journal.

8 Artist Adrian Piper, a friend of Rosemary's. They met while attending the School of Visual Arts from 1967–69.

Wed. Jan. 27 9:30 PM

Yesterday Bed & Board—silly easy—funny. Mon. peace at home reading. Tonight too excited. I'm so groggy from sleeping crazy to be alone & quiet. Sun. Vito's Birthday party. Totally hated Willoughby Sharp but then I was hardly in the mood for another night out. Sat. at 181 St. & Riverside Drive at Linda & Fred's dinner party. It was, strange enough, fun & I enjoyed it. It would be interesting if John Mudd young millionaire's son psychiatrist called me. I am truly off Phillip.

I need to clean this place up & feel still & ready to make the next piece. Abt. art I wonder...if I lived in Colorado married to John Mudd would it still be impt. to me to make the kind of that I do—is what I do diminished by its relation to the chain of high art—but I'm being led around by what people say—& who? Casey—Jack Burnham?

I doubt most people would see my stuff as a reaction to F Stella's "objects" & materiality & as a kind of "process art"—But it does bother me that it fits those last two categories so neatly—even though few people would see it. Both John & Casey said what I do is opaque. At first I was relieved bec. I thought it was too simplemindedly clear. But now I wonder if anybody would understand. I need more people to talk to who make things. John said it was ugly which really made me happy. I feel locked in in this stifling lack of heat—parched air—

I guess now that I think about it—If I were to make art—this art is what I would do—rich or poor—to sell or not.

I have to do something abt. $. There's no more & bills to pay. & Vito to repay. Hmmm.

3 plants have died so far from the winter.

I feel strong urges for cigarettes lately & also for liquor. Totally unsexy. Tired of having to look good—

Being alone like this I cannot eat, sleep at 5PM, take the phone off the hook—but then no one sees me in my good forms. Good & bad in everything.

They're talking abt. food on Channel 13. Food is one of the imp. things to me.

List of imp. things: not in order—Sunshine—Looking Thin Enough—Doing Good Work—Food—Being Peaceful Inside—Having Good Books to Read—A Few Good People—

Today I ate & drank—Espresso & Eggs—My Bread with Almond Butter—an apple—coffee—rose hips tea—yogurt w. preserves—1/2 lb. (yes) of fresh mozzarella—cranberry juice—espresso—a small potatoes w. butter—oh yes a cup of warm milk.

It's Chinese New Year—the year of the (suckling?) pig.

I need a full length mirror. And some clothes. I should make some w. Hannah's material. I want a long coat.

MONEY—It's probably a year I've been wondering what to do abt. $.

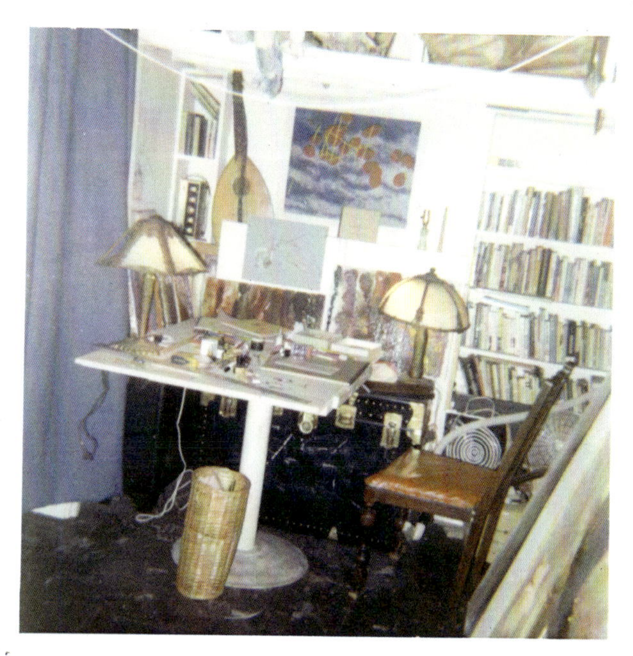

Sun. Jan. 30

Money still. Vito suggested I go away & teach at a little college. Being without friends like that frightens me. Maybe the best thing would be to teach at some progressive NY high school in Sept.—but figure a way to get out of here for the summer.

Tues. I'll go up to SVA. Wed. to the library for names of schools. Also this week write a resume—Get a usable typewriter.

So today I can have a clear head for other things I want to get all the annoying thoughts out. I need a new page—

Maybe I really do like it here in the NY Art World. The thought of leaving upsets me—bec. I really do want to be famous—that's awful but true—bec. I need friends around me who know me well—how would I deal w. not knowing where anything is, finding a big place to work, not having a car? If I am this uptight abt. it it's not time to do it. A summer away would do it & make it possible to stay here next winter. How to get away for the summer? Pay the current bills? If only I could sell something.

Tues. Feb. 2–Wed. 2 AM

I need a bigger space to work in...

I'm so fucking tired. I (didn't) sleep at John's last nite to avoid the cold. But I couldn't sleep. A bath was great & clean clothes—John's red undershirt—undershirts are great ideas.

John Perreault event was terrible.[9] Hannah said it was events beginning w. each letter of the alphabet. She took me out to dinner tonite. I'd called her & invited her down to see what I did w. her tricot. She liked it.

Philip Glass's concert last nite was terrific. Nobody could clap after it. His music is my favorite. Then last nite at John's I heard the Cage prepared piano music—another kind of great thing to hear.

John's going to read Silence. Good talks will follow.

Sunday was in a terrible mood—over $ & being alone. Monday dead tired bec. of Lucy Lippard at 9:15 AM. Couldn't tell what she thought. Today exhausted. And mad at the cats—they broke the TV aerial & the iron—quite a toll for 1 day.

Despite the cold, being tired & depressed I thought up a few new pieces today at work. One is really fine. A second is pretty good too. It's weird how ideas come.

Tonite Hannah & I talked abt. the being famous thing—how it's not that simple—part of it is a need to have yourself recognized for what you are—a creative artist—hmmm—before it sounded better &

9 *Alphabet*, performed at the Emanuel YMHA on January 31.

dif.—now it just sounds like ego gratification again...whc. I guess is nice. Is it just Catholicism that makes it seem wrong to want to be famous—that's not it though to be famous—it's to be surer of myself & my work—I'm beginning to be one of those people who lives & breathes art.

Mon. Feb. 8

STONED TIRED HEADACHE
Wed. NYU Snow Serra Nauman movies.[10] Just OK.
Thurs. a Woman's Lib. meeting—simpleminded & surfacy.
Fri. til Sun. a short Vito visit, a short Matthew visit.
Alone. Did another piece—paint is the glue. Not happy with work.
Last week's discontent has intensified. It's just not good enough.

Talked w. Phillip. Fri. He said maybe you just don't like me anymore. He was rt. Though I couldn't admit it then. I can't decide whether to see him again at all for a while—I guess it would be better to see him once more than to end it on the phone. He thinks he's too perfect. I hate his choice of words.

Down to 140 ½. GOOD. WOULD LIKE TO GET TO 135. IS IT POSSIBLE? FEEL THIN AGAIN.

Tonight John said "you go thru no smoking... no eating... so why not no men..." as though it were only logical... anyway it was funny.

I made terrible cookies this week & some very severe cornbread. I think I've been living on the cookies.

Reading S. Geidon Space, Time, and Architecture. It was really bad about the Renaissance but got into the 19th century.

Phillip is prob. one of the few men I will meet who is intellectually my equal. Vito & Charles & John. Is that snobby?

Vito came over to see work before he went to Nova Scotia. He did a

10 A series of performances and films called "Body," presented by John Gibson at New York University. This program is also mentioned on page 51.

good piece abt. being scared of going there. And another good one abt. revealing secrets on a pier at night.

Reading F.L. Wright On the Future of Architecture. All this naturalness of materials sounds like a paper I wrote in SVA 2nd Year class...where have I gotten since then? Better pieces—same ideas—but it seems to me most artists (past) had a few central ideas & all their works played w. those ideas. It's still true of Oldenburg—Stella—maybe even Warhol—all of Warhol is like a store—Staring at obj. or being stared at by them (or people). Only people in conceptual art keeping skipping along—& maybe that only seems to be true—Vito still transposes...accomplishes feats... The 2 new ones are dif.—self-revelatory art—

Tues. Feb. 9 5:15

the ROARS of TRUCKS

My retreat is working. I feel good again today. But tired. I've been sleeping a lot lately. Funny prickles in my head.

Bought A Year from Monday. Good. Again.

Robert Ryman's white paintings at Fischbach—an environment of whites. Not seen as separate paintings or as a group of paintings. Just lots of white. Upstairs—waxed paper's commonality I liked—All kinds of painterly goos. I gave up in 2nd year SVA bec. I thought of that sort of work as indulgence in loveliness for its own sake & nothing more. Using all white is really nice. So that you focus on the swirls & textures & stuff. The white room really made an impression on me, the upstairs is not so much. All that white—it seemed like it would be a good place to think or to live...clearing to the mind & senses. Is that really true or is it bec. of education that I believe that? Or is how I am now really true?

He got some of the pieces stuck to the wall w. paint—as in my new piece the grey paint holds the transp. stuff there.[11] Vito said how the lavender fabric is really just presentation—ground—and I felt the rug being pulled under—why hadn't I considered that—but is it true? The grey stain has to be on something—the wall? W. just the transparent stuff? Somehow that doesn't interest me the way two kinds of draping in one piece do—as opp. to red & blue piece where 2 pieces drape the same way—paint accents drapery.

11 Rosemary is referring to the first work in her *Veils* series, which involved layering different fabrics and painting on them. The work is shown on page 45.

2/16

The thing's up in the Cultural Center.[12] My nerves are shot between worrying how it would get done & having to get up early & not be able to sleep late after not being able to go to sleep. All day yest. was recovering—today an incredible headache—but it's up—a little crooked—that's the new esthetic problem.

My first thought on seeing it was how it reminded me of Eva Hesse—then no...the colors and stuff made it all too delicate—the crookedness—? I really didn't intend it—but I guess it's OK—it would just be usual art if it was all neat—It's funny how in my place—funky place—it looked edge-neater—& there in that pristine space it looks funky—the cheapness of everything in it—cord—knots—it blows in the air currents—but beautiful—

It's a dif. kind of funk than that current—of rubber & wooden & plastic guck—I think it's very much my own in its materials.

It might be too lovely if it were straight.

Lately I feel like I've been ineffectual—I haven't solved the job $ problem or the who's next prob. & now I'm beginning to think I need a bigger work space.

TREMORS OF MY FORMER SELVES

S. Geidion about "feeling" & emotion as the province of art & rationality of science, the latter being fully developed but people

12 Rosemary participated in an exhibition at the New York Cultural Center called *One Man One Work,* a series of small solo shows lasting two weeks. Each artist got to choose the person who exhibited after them. Sol LeWitt chose the first artist, Robert Jacks, who chose John Campione, who chose Adrian Piper, who chose Rosemary.

being pretty inept at "feeling." Art-feeling???

Preferences—Choices—but feeling?

Insights.

Veils, *Winter–Spring 1971*

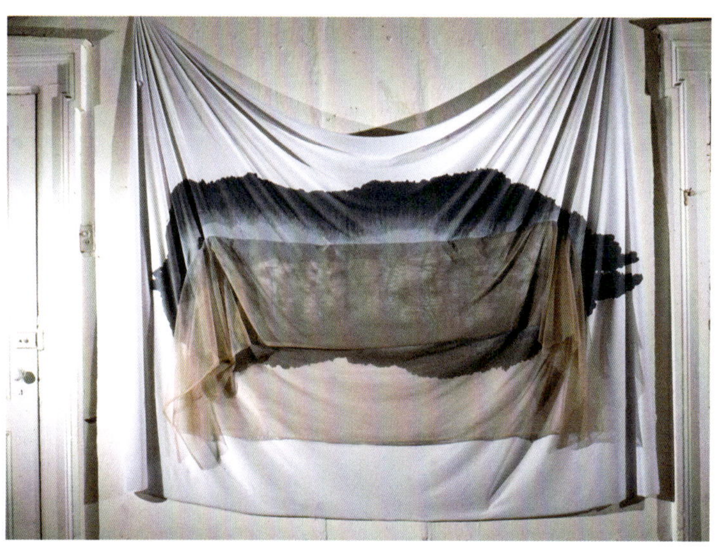

Veils I, February 1971. Nylon, tricot, and oil paint. Approximately 9 ft × 7 ft.

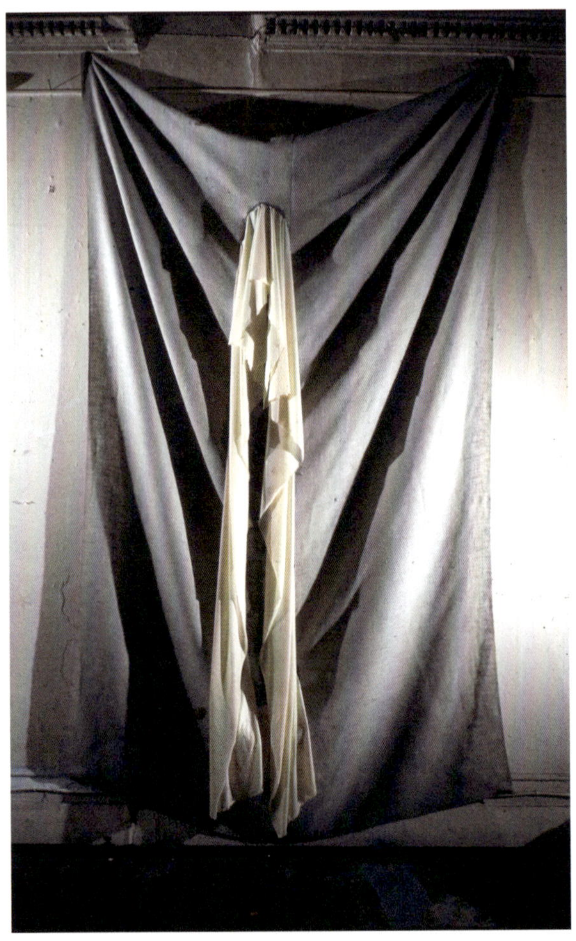

Veils II, 1971. Burlap and nylon. 10 ft × 6 ft.

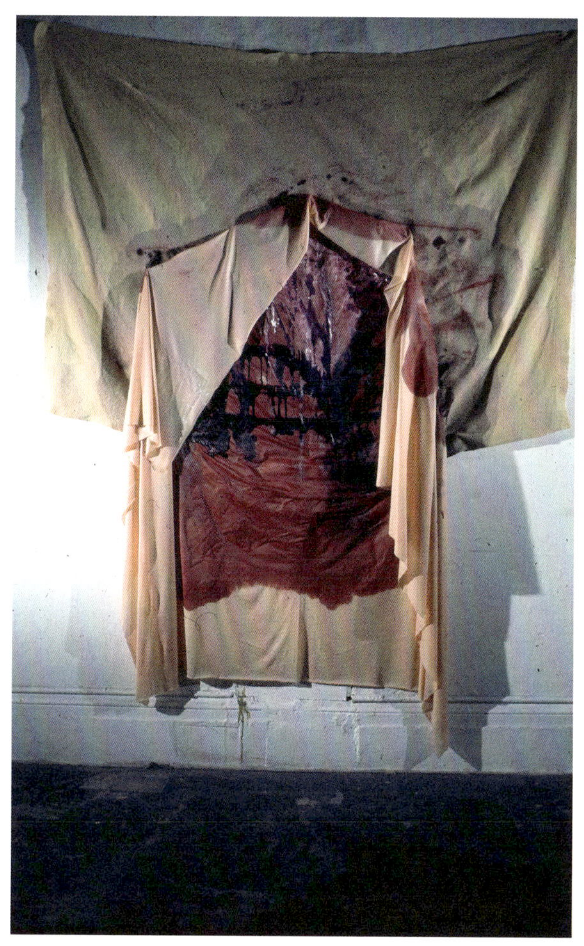

Veils III, 1971. Materials unknown. 8.5 ft × 8 ft.

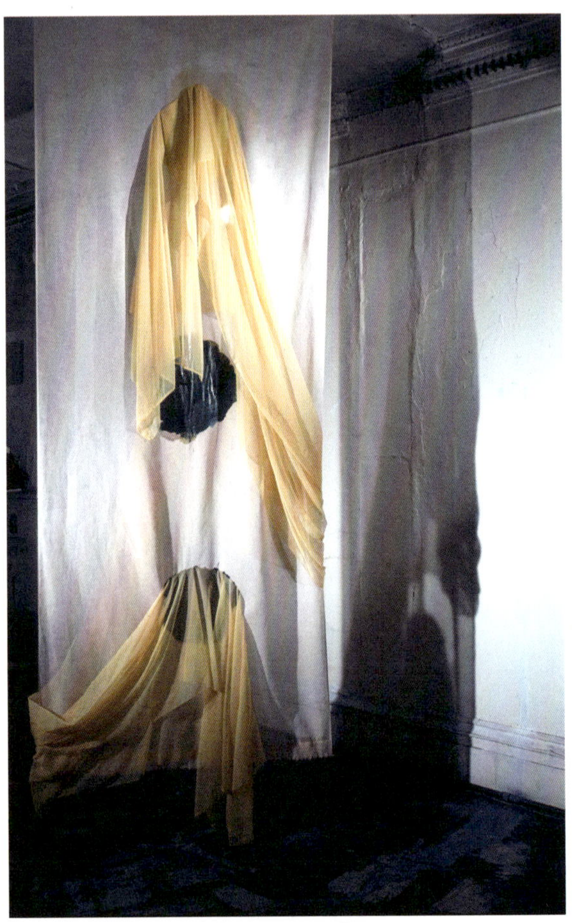

Veils IV, 1971. Voile, nylon, and enamel paint. 11 ft × 45 in.

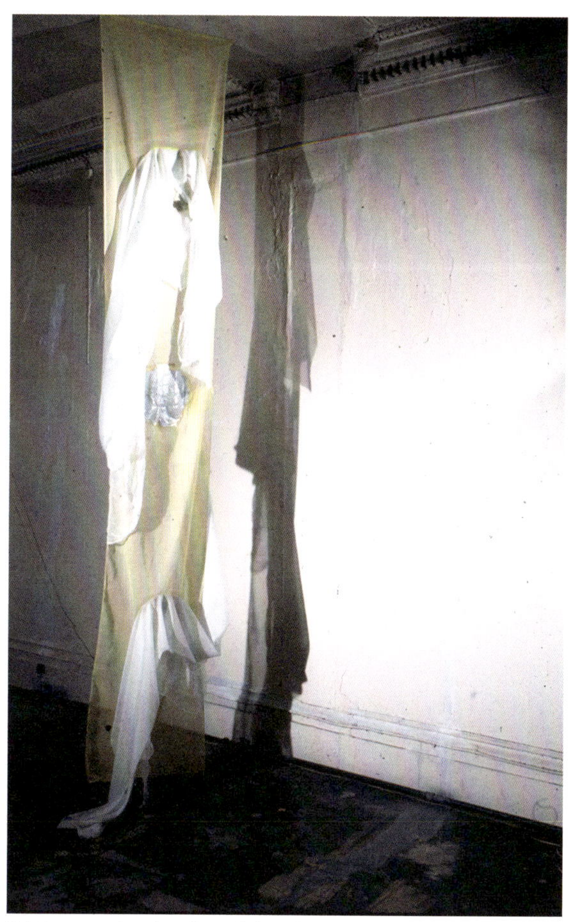

Veils V, 1971. Voile, nylon, cheesecloth, and oil paint. 11 ft × 23 in.

2/21 Sun. really Mon. 2AM

Sat. walking around figuring out the piece I did finally late Sat. nite & worrying about asking the landlord to store paintings upstairs. Too much coffee tho & the combination had me ready to pass out a few times. Sat really wore me out.

Woke up today w. a headache. Went out. Mistake—the air made it worse. Hannah was supposed to come for dinner & John but I really didn't want her to... & she called up sick... I called Adrian to come over & eat with us & she said no she was watching Jane Eyre on TV. Unbelievable.

Yest. I guess I dec. I have to go to work full time & I guess it's best to ask Jerry if I can work there.

Thurs. Steve Reich rehearsal. Didn't like the music too much & Phillip was less likeable than last Sat.

I guess I could use someone new for a lover. But it seems like an impossibility. It's too much trouble—for what? To find in the end a Phillip?

2/22

People—lots of people at J Gibson's NYU movies. Bernadette makes me feel overly serious.[13] Vito says they don't need any $ this month. So—no job for me—it's ludicrous how I worry and then don't worry—next month I'll be able to save $120—& need it all w.o. paying Con Ed or phone—but I could pay them not pay loan—so—I can't face 9–5 5 days—I know it—I'll keep looking for some faster less straight $.

Too many movies tonight. Vito's seemed innocent & not contorted and ugly as when I've heard abt. them.

13 Rosemary's younger sister, Bernadette Mayer, often abbreviated as "B" in the journal. Primarily a poet, she had co-edited with Vito Acconci *0 TO 9*, the journal of experimental art and writing, from 1967 to 1969. In July of 1971, she created *Memory*, an ambitious work that involved shooting a roll of film and writing in a journal everyday for a month. She exhibited the project at Holly Solomon's gallery the following year, in an installation consisting of 1,100 snapshot photographs mounted in a grid and six hours of audio recordings based on her journals.

3/1—2:30 PM at work

What Happened This Weekend—Thurs. nite I made my cake & some terrible bread. Fri. nite Phillip & Adrian & Dave came over. It wasn't scintillating but it was OK…

Sat. on the way to lunch with Mary, met Adrian who brought me a Bird of Paradise—Lunch OK—I really like Mary.[14] She gave me a little plant. Then I went to help John—Ethelyn Honig—then went to Chez Brigitte & his house—where Casey was & drank beer & talked. Then we went to Linda's. She had a cake for me & a plant too. I was really surprised.

Sun. I & John missed each other at 29 W. 26 & I went to his place—found Casey—finally John—went to LC to hear Stockhausen[15]—which was just OK—went to John's & drank beer and got stoned with Casey—went to Adrian's & home. I cooked a great mushroom omelet, fresh coleslaw, & macaroni & cauliflower—all unexpected & unplanned. I surprised myself. We watched To Catch a Thief. John & I fell asleep.

I enjoyed all the running around. I didn't want to be home this weekend. I wanted lots of people—& I got it—

I had prob. the best Birthday I remember—$ is the problem—that's all—

14 Mary Hilgeman, a friend from St. Joseph's College.

15 This performance of Karlheinz Stockhausen took place at Lincoln Center, part of a series of experimental music called "New and Newer Music."

3/9 Tuesday 7:30 PM

I feel almost without mood. Tired of thinking I'm bored. A new piece is on my mind. Macy's tom. AM I've got to get up & Roger Corman films after work. Though I see people almost every day I feel very solitary—but not too bad abt. it. Moving the furniture was a good idea bec. it keeps me reminded of writing & reading & thinking I want to do.

Reading J Cage is disturbing. I think of what is relevance of what I do to the world?

There's so much to do.

3/10

Abt. galleries & being in one contributing to a retrograde form when everyone should be an artist:

1) everyone would not be a good artist—
2) I should get $ for what I do so I can do more of it
3) I have something to show people

Materials today—the colors too lush—too likeable—no one needs to do anything more to them—

Donna Dennis—sweet & shy & under wraps.[16] We'll mate our cats. She's very attractive. Those beautiful blue eyes.

Art pushes the boundaries where afghans & scarves & pillowcases don't. Could they?

16 Close friend and fellow artist, often abbreviated as "D".

3/11/71

Smell of that green & grey metal children's lunch case I had in grammar school when I opened it up—sandwiches wrapped in Cut Rite waxed paper—and apples

old smells
old stuff with old textures

the smell especially of ham sandwiches—

on something like Taystee bread—

Donna last nite—an innocent—not like me

Anne's poetry innocent while B's is not—like me[17]

B should put maps of the N & S pole on her book for its covers—or maybe clouds—bec. the book is her world—a sign for it as the map is a sign for the world.[18]

Donna said last nite that she kept thinking my cats were her cats with different clothes on.

I have to concentrate more on me. For somebody who has no obligations to anyone I'm surprisingly other oriented.

17 Anne is possibly the poet Anne Waldman.

18 This is likely Bernadette Mayer's book *Moving*, which was published later that year and included drawings by Rosemary in the interior. The cover was designed by Ed Bowes, Bernadette's boyfriend at the time, and ultimately incorporated a photograph of Bernadette.

3/13 Sat.

Vito, John, Casey & Kathe, another Cathe, Roger Corman, a party & me & Casey talking here. Casey makes me feel good—talking about art. I think Corman is good—I think talking about art is a sex surrogate.

3/14

Sunday with a hangover. Sick last nite. How close to myself I feel when I'm sick.

A tremendous urge to fit neatly into some category—like someone's girlfriend—

The boy cat is chasing leaves—dry leaves that crackle

I mostly slept this weekend. Fri. nite I did some drawings w. crayons. The Cage concert was good & I'm glad Phillip didn't come. I no longer feel there's more liking on his end than on mine.

Mary said I ought to tell John how I've been wanting him. It's prob. bec. I feel that w. his girls he's liking me less. Whc. isn't true since we're on the phone tog. all the time. I have to stop expecting him to pay for things. He works for $ too.

I really feel that I drove myself this week—to read and use time instead of being lazy. And what did it get me—needing to sleep all day Sat. practically.

Maybe one shld. laze around until you can't anymore—Should—is so bad a way to be.

The Quiller Memorandum is on TV. It's absorbing me.

I can't believe all this time w. no sex & no urges. The wanting John isn't really sex. Exactly what? Unity w. him for a while—to possess him.

I have a real craving for milk & oranges.

I wonder what to do with the crayons.

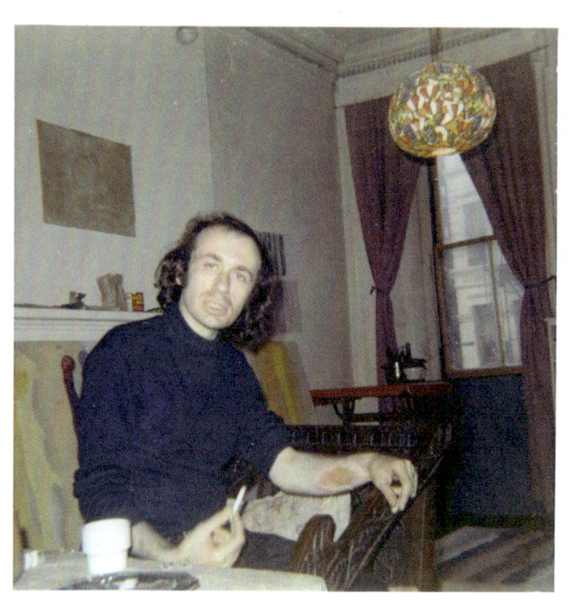

3/16 Tues.

A dinner cooked for John—which he will pay for—I'm that poor—I felt fine today until I walked home—Now my head is clogged. I called Curtis this AM & he is coming down here Mon. the 29—He-He—I worried at work (but only a little) abt. what to do if they go bankrupt. Call Raphael & get unemployment.[19]

I make 3D Morris Louis'? Met Vito on the way home & we talked abt. Colin Cherry, J Burnham (whose verbiage we both can't get thru & whom we both suspect—as we would suspect all one truth systems.)

I've got to get Levi-Strauss to read... $ or not...

I think after all this reading I ought to write some criticism.

John...yest. I wanted him—today I don't or is it defense so that I'll be unaffected if I don't get him—?

Something's changed bec. I shaved my legs.

I could prob. live totally wrapped up in art. If I were rich...would I try to get into a gallery?...def. I would buy art...& so I would know more artists...or dealers...what incredible end of worries...to have $...

When did I last buy something new to wear—Last Mar. when I bought that white outfit? & red shoes...?? Last Nov. when I bought my Navy pants...

I ought to write a commentary on the art scene...in a sep. book...

19 Raphael Soyer (1899–1987) was primarily a painter known for his portraits and scenes of New York. Rosemary modeled for him for many years and he became a close friend. Bernadette Mayer and Donna Dennis also modeled for him.

3/16/71 at work

John Cage Stories

abt. the

Last Twenty Four Hours

or

Rosemary & Con Edison

or

Vitamin B vs. the electricity

I've spent 24 hrs. doing very little but worry about when, where, with what and whether, I should pay Con Edison.

And after all the worry, this morning I conned Con Edison into an extension of the turn-off date.

To make myself feel better: this is a list of what other things I did manage to do: watched 1/2 of two movies, read 20 pages of Colin Cherry, talked to Mary, John & Andrea, watched Muhammad Ali on TV, put up the cheesecloth for the next piece. Made bread.

The materials for the next piece trouble me. Cheesecloth—but what else. After looking at the velvet it's not that. I wish I had more time to look at fabrics—

I also wonder where those drawings are going.

3/19 Fri.

UPSET OVER PROB. LOSS OF JOB. I shouldn't be so affected by it. Is it better to stay there or go full time & get fired?

Crayon drawings. Weds. I bought a piece of red fake silk looking stuff. I'm stuck w. that & the cheesecloth.

Why do I find it so hard to throw things out? Work I know is only pretty, old clothes, old pots & dishes??

Why do I always dream of places—bldgs.—rooms—??

Reading Burnham, Levi-Strauss & Colin Cherry. HARD WORK.

3/22

Yest.—1st day of spring—Weird experiences—no, really ordinary—but so revelatory of my easily led nature—Orchard St. to look at fabrics—the kind of people like Momma & Poppa—and then writing up my resume—academic memories—days when I thought being somebody great was not only imp. but my destiny. So I was a little shook bec. I felt as though I hadn't done anything—nothing published, no $—as though those things were still impt. to me now when I'm seriously doubting the rightness of my wanting to be a "great artist."

This is unclear, like my head this AM.

3/23 Tues.–Wed. Midnite

Now it's no more job. But it might (small chance) change. No thoughts of my work exc. wishing I could be sitting here thinking about it... reading without interruption... Instead 2 9–3 days of wondering what to do about $.

Today I went to an agency to see what it would be like—& I'm not sure what happened. The guy said to come back but when I said I could make a 3:30 appointment he just said call me or come back—Can I really stand a 9–5 job? If I can't—could I swindle myself some welfare $—? It's so boring & so necessary.

Phillip called. I still hate the ways he says some things but otherwise I feel better abt. him I guess.

This weekend I couldn't find anything to complete the red fake silk & the cheesecloth.

I haven't felt coherent today or yesterday—

Can shit work be good for your head—?? Casey at Woolworth's.

The cats are good—to hug—& fondle—& they're so cute—I could eat them.

4/4

So much has gone on in the last 2 weeks—& I've not felt it esp. necessary to write it down—my head has been going round & round.

Last weekend I made a red & cheesecloth piece & it was pretty terrible—

Mon. Curtis came over & said he liked things & I should show him more when I had them. I feel pressured & worried I won't have any more ideas. I hated being the little officiant.

Drawings

Other topic—JOB—SEX—LONELINESS—the coming SUMMER

John & Donna—[20]

20 Rosemary's friend and sometimes lover John started dating a woman named Donna, different than Donna Dennis who she meets earlier this year and becomes a very close friend.

4/16

I'm not pregnant—a test thru Dr. M—negative—a real scare—day dreams of what I would have done if I had been—a job in a week for $120—He-He—but a full time job—UGH

A new piece—on Tuesday—an abortion—red as blood.[21] I don't know. V & K of course liked it.

Another one started today.

I guess I'll survive working—20 weeks is til the beg. of Sept. for all those months of no work—

The red piece confused me—it's good to push at boundaries—& it certainly pushes at my taste's boundaries—but...

21 This is the third work in the *Veils* series, which Rosemary sometimes titled *The Abortion*. Shown on page 47.

April 23—Friday at work at quarter to 11

I wish I had a nice pen to write this with. There's a great deal to catch up on. Ardrey says one's needs are, first, identification within the group; second, sex & third, security. Let's get the third over first.

The number of feelings I've gone thru this week—first getting myself used to the idea of a full-time job & then switching around & getting the nerve to go collect illegal unemployment.[22] I hope it works. Thoughts of all the things I would buy if I had $ from a regular job—iron, typewriter, desk lamp—full-length mirror—clothes maybe—but it's truly not worth it to work for things—they'll come—it's boring to write about all this bec. I've thought of it so much—

As for work—it is going good—I want to be doing more—I'm not sure the colors in the new piece aren't too acceptably lovely to be interesting—and it's going to take weeks to let 3 enamel stains dry. John gave me some good heavy paper—I want to use it to find a way to play w. colors—look for good ones w. my gouaches, pastels—it seems that my sensibility has moved from the def. applied textures of winter 69–70 to the textures in stuff. That's a good move. I wonder abt. my drawings. I want to be doing another piece now. Maybe to do the red & cheesecloth again—Something with cheesecloth. It would be good I think to go back to materials after I've looked at what I've already done & how the stuff did.

It's incredible how one's feelings swing back and forth. When I was sure I had to work—the thought of getting dressed every day was horrid. Now today I found me wondering if I missed getting all

22 Rosemary collected unemployment benefits during the year, which she mentions frequently, and it seems to have been a source of stress. She sometimes abbreviated it as "UE."

cleaned up & feeling smooth & dressed up.

I wonder if dirty old Broome St. will get to me. I'll need a fan. I should be able to afford one w. reaḷ economy next month. I'll be able to do all those things I did last year—when I had lots of time—water the plants, stare at them, keep the place clean (well, cleaner), sit in the sun—read, daydream, sleep enough, write in my book, do exercises, cook cheap food—plus beach, Massachusetts.

I wonder about food stamps.

I wish there was a way to get to the roof from the back of the building—but who'll see me anyway in 5 minutes climbing—go up there & read—sleep—

I should cut my pair of pantyhose to shreds—& mail them to who's responsible for people having to work—

Meditating another diet—to fit into those old pants fr. SVA—But I have been since Jan. Cigs. are becoming a problem again—probably bec. of wondering what's up w. $—

To get completely immersed in my thoughts my rhythms—though this job hasn't been such a disturbance—but then I'm good at staying undisturbed—am I? what about all this mental clutter about jobs & unemployment? Now imagine how wretched to work 9–5—really I would have been leaving at 8:15—get back at quarter to 6—prob. being tired too—

John gave me a pink watch yesterday. He's bought himself an air conditioner & a big mattress—sex is on his mind I guess—he & Adrian think I'm foolish with my idealistic conceptions of the perfect affair—total communication, total trust—complete admiration—I ought to talk to Vito abt. it.

Going to the pier for Vito's piece was really an experience.[23] Terrors & really beautiful lights & water & clear heady air—I wish I could live there—

23 This may be Acconci's work, *Untitled Project for Pier 17*, which took place at an abandoned pier on the west side of downtown Manhattan.

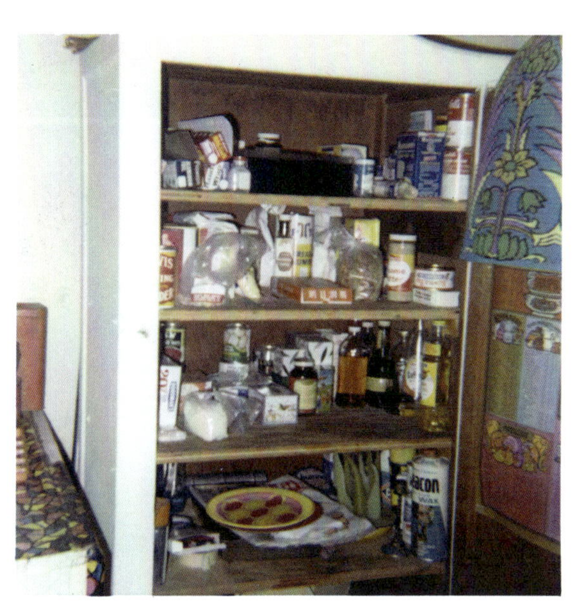
WAX

May 1

Knowing I don't have to go to work 1) is incredibly relaxing—I feel like I can take time to do things—like talk to people—read slower—ramble around in stores—think twice 2) makes me totally responsible—what now can prevent me doing what I want? No excuses—? weather? illness? No $? Can all be gotten around with time—

He-He—such a feeling of peace. I hope it works. I think I will put some paintings up at Cameo—& I'll visit R in 2 weeks after I sign for unemployment.

2 ideas for pieces. Somehow I'm bored with them after I think them up—I have to get more involved in the doing—I spend all myself thinking up how. I'm sure there are good ideas to catch in the doing.

A cat—the girl is holding onto my arm as I write. I had time to care for the plants today. I'm getting human again.

I already know it is nothing to have a show...but I feel like I can't give it up now...to sell things to decorate rich people's houses UGH—but to have $ to get doing what I want...but it is also pride...to have people know who I am...that I'm good at something...in part it would be getting back at people who ignore me...WOW... PRIDE...PRIDE... whc. is why I want such a perfect lover...but I can see no good in being humble...what is it good for to be satisfied w. what is already...to not try to be better...do more...be famous even...

5/6–7 1 AM

Abt. work... KK is over my shoulder but that should be over in a week.

The weather is getting warmer. This year I'm not interested in the sunshine & the air. It's all too poison... I'd rather exercise inside. John bought an air conditioner... a good idea.

I wonder what to do abt. drawings... abt. paint surface on my pieces—I don't like thick muck of rosygold or the very stretched out thinness of the newest NAVY ORANGE GREY piece either. A good goal would be the inbetween.

Nothing is so important—not everyday some chores to do rush around breathing fast... I have to be careful I don't gain weight. I wish I'd get up earlier. Set the clock far away...

I wonder... in my pieces there definitely is the idea that paint doesn't belong on those fabrics... automatic violence which is increased by how uncomfortable the paint looks there... how it doesn't go with the lovely soft or luxurious fabrics... in the NOG one there's the contrast between the grey burlap alone & how it's revealed through the blue & the paint—Maybe that only makes sense to me.

5/15

When I talked to B she said nothing abt. my drawings.

Everything seems blunted & sterile. I feel numb & empty. I feel there are countless things abt. which I have no clear idea. I'm esp. troubled by the textures in paint that have been turning up in my work. I don't know what to do abt. them.

Howard too said nothing abt. my pieces...

If I weren't taking all that Vitamin B I'd prob. be crazy—dull giving up crazy

I've not been very hungry lately. I never want to cook anything.

Topics to write about keep popping into my mind.

Conversations—with Raphael—with B tonite—Onibaba—The Grapes of Wrath & S Peckinpah last nite—why I'm not more observant—John & what I've gotten from him—Phillip—my dreams the last 2 days so rooted in unimportant visual events—

Raphael discounting abstraction—"to make a whole art of a minor part of painting..." I'm a purist...subject matter is extraneous—it is the materials & their properties that I love...J. Pollock is so important & Louis...I have to find ways to use more paint.

Raphael also saying how one ought to participate in demonstrations...he is right abt. that...I am being just cowardly.

B talking abt. how she wants not to be distinct with her preserve of a thing to do but to be more involved with the real world. The real world frightens me. It's dull & vicious.

Vito has got past materials into a subject matter...have I? I'm making materials my subject matter.

Onibaba seemed very roughly pieced together which was good because it's different...but very overdone in the crudeness of the people.

The Grapes of Wrath I liked. I had thought I would think it pathetic & sentimental...but it wasn't...though I couldn't say I was moved.

S Pekinpah's The Deadly Companions was rambling almost no story where activities became more important than the goals—& there were many goals—rob a bank, get vengeance, bury a boy—but all-in-all simpler & more obvious than his later films.

John has made me more hesitant to get involved in anything. That's not good.

I wish I knew some people who made things.

Today I feel I'm still shy & inhibited bec. H said would I like to come to a play P Glass' wife is in & I wouldn't because those people make me nervous.

Sunday 5:40 PM [May 16]

Talking last night with H abt. A Nin's Diary... it is so sure of her own goodness. We tore it apart for words like goodness & truth. We said it was too poetic & delicate. Reading today abt. her psychoanalysis it seems more real. Why do I think it's imp. for it to be real... She seldom talks abt. her body exc. to regret its delicacy. She never mentions its smells, or aches, or her sex life...

H said there is no reason to be upset by feeling pulled in dif. directions. We decided what you feel you need to do at a time is valid for then. There is no reason to think that if I went off living w. someone I would not do my work & my wanting that kind of life doesn't invalidate my work. There's no need to be single-minded...

A man would never think that love would make it impossible for him to do other things he wanted. It's just me feeling unable to handle two complexities.

AN's description of her submissive obed. Catholic childhood struck home. So did her conviction that it had undermined her self-confidence & made her submissive to men as a way of absolving her of responsibility for herself. SO TRUE.

Also her assumption of a mask to avoid being hurt. Only her mask was goodness, sweetness, etc., whereas mine is assurance, intellect, work, seriousness. She too created a warm soft comfortable home as a serene retreat.

Massachusetts May 20 around Midnight

In the hottest bathtub. It's almost as good as sex. But it's a little hard to breathe.

I came away bec. staying at Broome St. all the time was getting out of control. I was either incessantly doing things or in a stupor in front of the TV. This mostly at night until 2:30 or 3:30 AM. I have to get back to my ability to be alone and be peaceful. Maybe thinking abt. it up here will help.

I've decided to give freer reign to my feelings. I'm always tucking them away to keep them out of my way.

Mass. Fri. 11:30 PM [May 21]

Here I am in C & K house with the rain outside and they're on their way to VT. I've been thinking about sex for most of the day. Sex & art.

My stomach feels terrible. I'm eating Swiss cheese & a yeasty. I ought to fast tomorrow.

Tonite I will empty my head into this book & tom. I could empty my body w. liquids till sunset. Also I should go & meditate in the woods after the rain has washed everything clear.

I feel like I'm having another adolescence—why at this point. It must be because a change is going on—the time of cautious self-sufficient solitude is over. The change time—NOW—is ripping me up. What next? I'm after more involvement with people, more art making—but fewer certainties—faster change.

This afternoon I went to the pine grove near the little pool. Lots of mosquitoes. But a pine needle carpet. Many greens. Bird sounds & the creaking of bending trees. Also the wind in all the trees. I felt very peaceful. I woke up that way today & going there made it more so. I found some lovely stones. The peace was what I've been looking for—for weeks—

A Nin talking to Otto Rank—how women are closer to the child, the artist, the primitive. How creative women we know abt. have become like men—in that image.

"You replace the last object of your love by imitating him."

—the urges to live like Vito, or like B—the only lives I know intimately—how they wake up, wash, brush hair, eat etc.—

Making my art seems like such a physical impossibility—too much dirt, things never dry, you never know how they will act, I rush thru it—I hate having to buy all the parts every time—

To have a big clean bright place—space & more thought abt. each piece—

Plus where is all the knowledge—astrology, myths, magic, feelings, that my work now doesn't allow?

Pages from Sketchbook, May–June 1971

45"

3 yds

this one thin

this one thick + glueing

1 heavy

1 transparent

Tonite very depressed abt stuff — Since Jan —
9 pieces — overlays, abortion, sonic pouring all
terrible. Sonic pouring is destroyed. that leaves 6
in 5 months — and its still the same idea —
PAINT AS GLUE — DRAPING — TRANPARENT FABRICS
TO SHOW PAINT UNDERNEATH —
I want to get into more PAINT

Letting stuff do what it will — Morris' Antiform article
M. LOUIS
J. POLLACK

GRAVITY

Pouring —

dont even feel like bothering to do this
ne) — bec it doesn't seem that dif

PAINT is the way out of remaking R. Morris' Antiform
Pieces — + the way into ILLUSIONS ←
I really want to investigate that?

ON WHAT
ATTACHED HOW?

PAINT
DRIPPING
thru
Broken
skins

Colors
stuff
SIZE

Thin

thick

REMEMBER - THICK THREAD

5/30

white space

black

To let yellow marks show

more space

6/1 many discussions lately w. many people.

Vito said they are all pretty =. This mbe what A means when she says formal inovation is pointless. A's attitude annoys me: how they are too pretty — + not as angry as I. I dont think Im esp. angry — ~~they are~~ Some of them are too pretty — only the ROSYGOLD I think though — Hannah says their loveliness is fine — she likes it bec it is how these materials are. I think of its use in using this stuff — draping fabric will always be lovely — H says Vito + C liking the Abortion is perverse. I think making these things on purpose ugly w. be perverse — + bad art — A also agrees w. how symmetrical they are — V too thinks this is a drawback — I wonder how to go about thing w.o. that structure. — By making them symetrical one passes over ~~the~~ placement decisions — + I can concentrate on their materials —

yellow polyester like in 2nd last piece + yellow satin

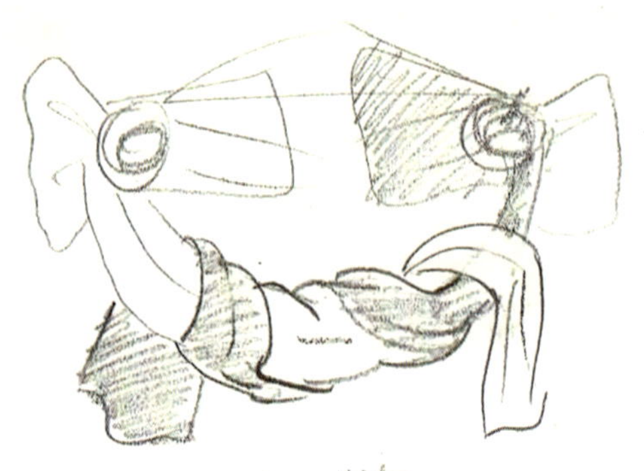

awfully complicated

maybe for once I should buy some stuff & just
play w it – but how to know how much
very fine limp stuffs – nylon – polyester –

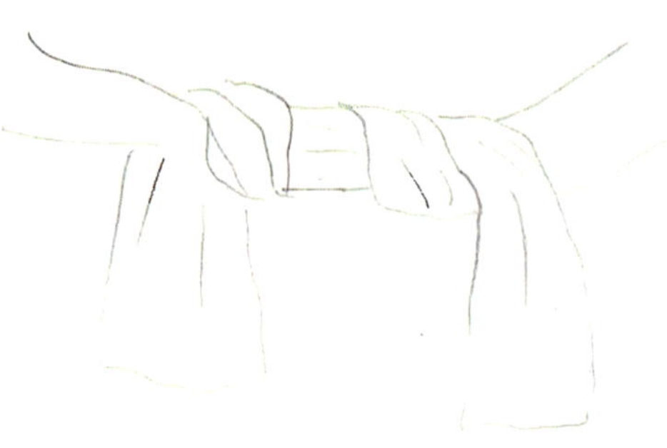

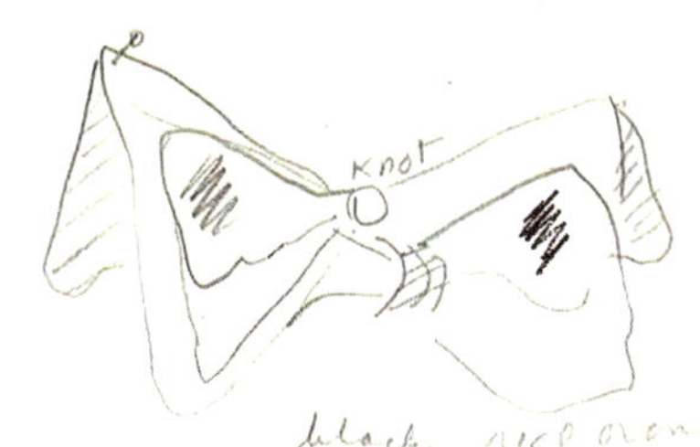

3 materials black, yel orange, pale blue purple
slightly not symmetrical

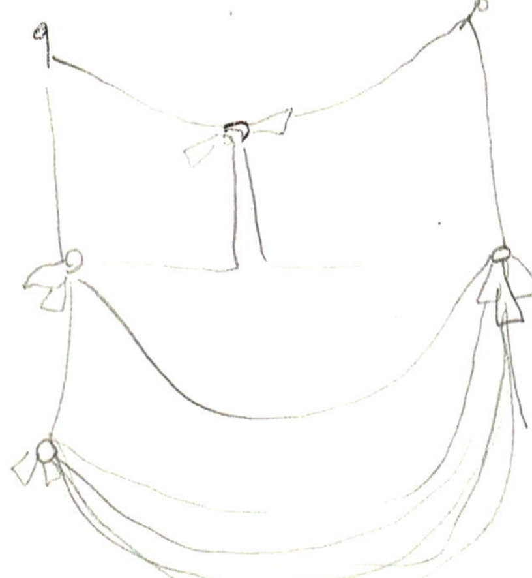

all knotted piece

Nobody seems very excited —
what next — More knots?—

6/12

3 yds of 3 - top one transparent -

2 cheesecloths

glue

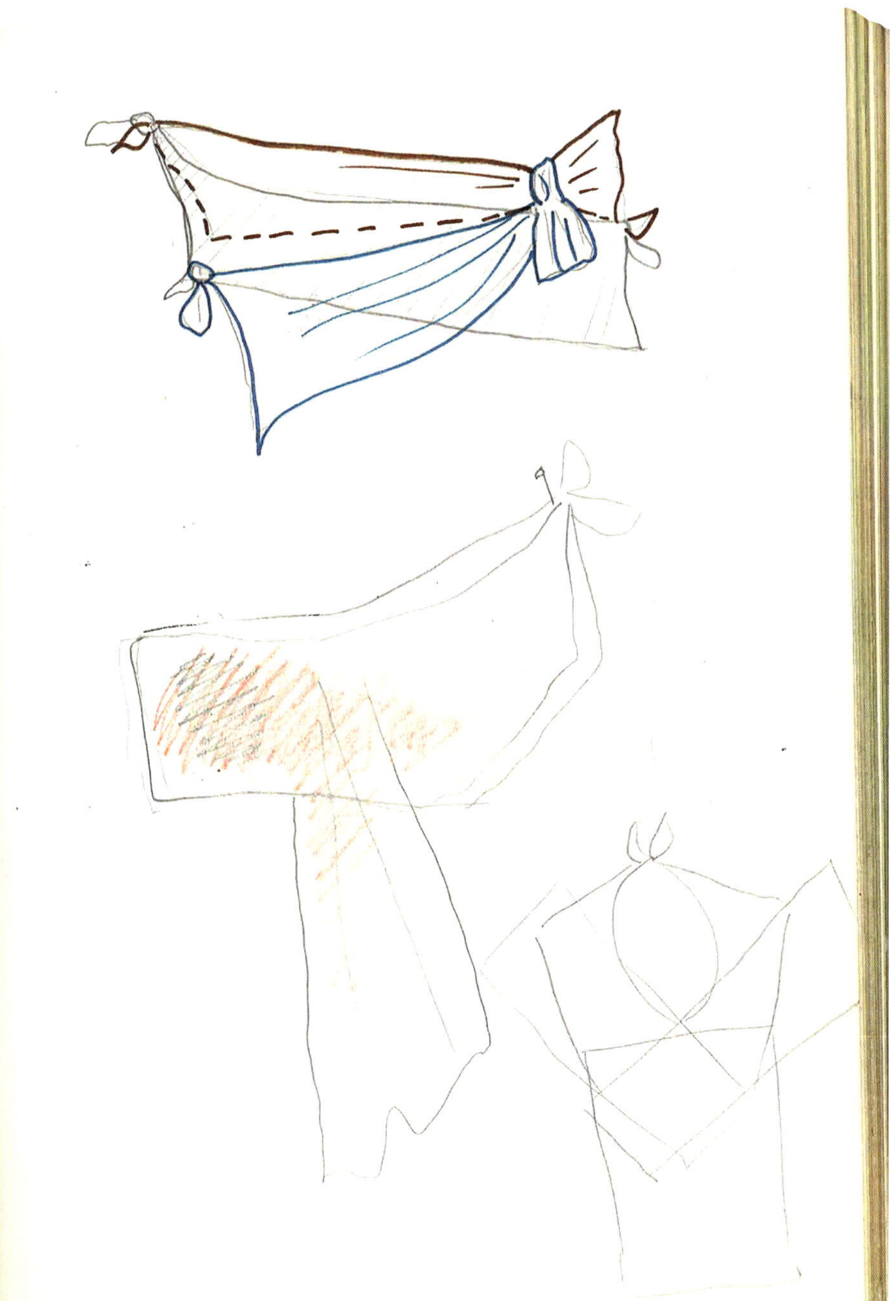

Tues. 9:50 [May 25]

The slow dullness of Mass. made it good to be back here. But last nite I was so unhappy abt. John & so worried abt. the Unemployment— But that worked—within 2 weeks—$—

SO now I feel it's time to clean—the house & me—Tomorrow— oranges & eggs and no more cigarettes—Getting up early in the AM—

I'm so tired today—2 hrs. of sleep last night and fitful sleep all afternoon. An incredible dream—

Talking to Adrian abt. the clash of brutal paint surfaces with lovely fabrics. She said how that's me—that my urge to make a middle ground is really a not good idea—I ought to accept the hard brutal parts of me—

2AM BEAUTY

SECURITY

EASE

SAFETY

Thurs.–Fri. 1 AM [May 27–28]

Falling apart—like I have no whole self as B has—no past together with future. B said when they all died it made her see there is no logic—what did I get from it?[24] A hard time with emotions—

I like the house again but I'll paint the floor & get a fan.

Howard's show made me feel I ought to write something. Statements abt. me—

My work seems so delicate & beautiful—isn't there enough beauty—I guess I really don't feel there is enough but it seems too easy a thing to do—

Look up all the words about beauty tomorrow

24 Rosemary and Bernadette's father died in 1957; their mother died in 1959. Rosemary was 14 and 16, respectively, at the time of their deaths.

Sat. 7 PM [June 5]

Today was quite a day for the emotions. Everybody else seems so low key to me. Except maybe Raphael when he was angry because it was late—& Roger smiling goodbye. I got depressed very early—abt. my worrying abt. being on time to model. Then R kept on abt. my being fat—& I got dep. at myself even considering that—I just have this incredible reaction to that word FAT. Then I went food shopping & bought corn, cucumbers, peaches & grapefruit & then at the supermarket milk, a coffee yogurt, string beans, veg. baked beans, butter, & ricotta cheese. I really wanted to make that list—the flavors of the beg. of this summer. Oh yes a can of mackerel for the cats. This summer—how will it be dif. than last year? I'm not so peaceful—nor do I feel so well. I feel pressured—fr. myself—to get my work moving—into some other place. Vito's piece at Greene Street was—I don't know—surrealistic—strangely peaceful—I had expected fighting and blood & instead he was sort of mothering them in this tiny, special place w. lots of mirrors—there was little motion & Vito when he moved, was slow & gentle.[25]

25 Rosemary is referring to *Combination*, which Acconci performed at 112 Greene Street on June 5, 1971. The performance consisted of Acconci naked in a space lined with mirrors and containing three roosters that he tried to cover himself with.

Mon. 10 AM [June 7]

Yesterday I set up things for myself to do—Make a new piece w. the leftovers, label the slides, write the questions—& I did them. Today I have no plans.

Donna came over yesterday. Being w her makes me nervous. Maybe I'm afraid I'm not appearing well enough.

I compete w my own image of myself.

I worked w the fabrics I dyed on Sat. Nothing seemed to work out. Knots & no paint.

I started to write just random sentences based around words I liked from the thesaurus.

I wish I could do some small works as Donna does her collages.

John called last nite. All the TV movies were terrible. I read some Sylvia Plath. I like her except sometimes there is too much of wounds and death.

Thurs. [June 10]

Mon. nite I saw H. Mostly we talked about people. A little abt. art. She is always curious abt. Vito. Tues. I went to Unemployment Office on very very little sleep & then at 10:30 or so back here John turned up. We went to the Cultural Center to see the English Avant-Garde of which only R Long was even OK. We saw Warhol's early shoes at Gotham Book Mart. Then we went to see Escape fr. the Planet of the Apes. The mythology of our time. Thousands of people knowing the same stories.

I got home at 8:30 or so—dead & started to watch TV. I was too tired to sleep & didn't til abt. 3—

Wed. morning I had to model so early up again. I went to Fischbach afterwards but they weren't looking at new work till the fall.[26] I came home feeling rotten. I bought a turtle. He won't eat. I cleaned up a little. I slept fr. 6 til 10 and watched all terrible movies. Then slept fr. 2 til 10.

The cats are confused abt. the turtle. I hope he doesn't die. The philodendron has 3 new leaves lately. The purple plant isn't well. Tonight there's a women's meeting.[27] Am apprehensive but curious enough to go.

26 Fischbach Gallery was another leading gallery, located on the Upper East Side. It showed the work of Eva Hesse, who was an influence on Rosemary, and also Robert Mangold, who had been her professor at the School of Visual Arts.

27 This seems to be the first mention of the consciousness-raising group that Rosemary participated in for a couple of years. Core members included Adrian Piper, Donna Dennis, Randa Haines, Jane Weiss, and Grace Murphy. Rosemary's sister Bernadette (referenced as "B") also attended a few meetings in the beginning.

PM 2:30 Friday June 11

Last nite's meeting was interesting to me…bec. I heard B in a new situation & I learned more abt. her than I have in a long time…She kept talking abt. how being an idealist should not be a comment but a step to other goals. She had no idea what should come next but just that things might be different & there should be something to do to change it all. I spoke very little except to comment on other people. I feel I had very little to say. I didn't think the evening was very interesting. But I'll go again in hopes of it getting better. There was wine to drink & had quite a bit & got a headache & slept very late today.

Yesterday was a busy day. The UE check finally came. I got it cashed in a check cashing place. I went & bought the Yoga book, some old magazines, the Russian Psychic Research Book, & went to Greenberg's for yeast, molasses, rose hips preserves, sesame butter & granola. I ate very little yesterday: tapioca, a yeasty, a little granola, a salad, some cheese & almonds, & wine & lemonade & coffee. 140 this AM—when, how will it get below. 5 lbs. would make me so happy. Tiny portions.

I want to read Heraclitus—bec. in the Yoga book the part abt. the truth being still & unchanging bothers me. I need activity. I can't yet start the exercises…maybe later today…or tomorrow…I also want to read more Thoreau…and do something with the magazines…I have no new ideas for pieces…

Tues. July 13

I feel strange. I've survived a really unpleasant heat wave—that lasted til last Sat. What terrible days. I took gigantic amounts of Vit. B bec. I was so depressed abt. being unable to move, think, or sleep. Sat. it got better. Sun. I went to Stokes Forest in NJ w. Mary & Michael. Getting out of here really improves my frame of mind. I felt mildly desperate on Sun.—like there was nothing happening w. me so why not run away—but I came back to a meeting & Mon. I felt better. Part of my feeling better came fr. the delightful weather—cool, sunny, & breezy, part of feeling better came fr. having enough to do to keep me busy. I went to see GP.[28] I shopped for dinner, I moved all the furniture & I cooked for John & Donna. But today there was nothing to do. I slept a lot—to make up for getting up early but more than I had to. There was nothing I wanted to do.

The meeting was OK. We didn't talk much abt. the topic—sexual feelings for other women but we talked at least. A lot of what gets said though I think everybody already knows & doesn't need to be said (but I guess someone needs to say it).

Part of my moving furniture yesterday was to put the mattress on the floor. Which was a good idea. Cool & I do exercises bec. the mattress is right there. I did yoga today... HOORAY. When I next need food... pure stuff.

What to do? I need things to read. I have to try The Raw & the Cooked.

28 GP was Rosemary's grandfather who was in poor health.

Fri. July 16

Wed. Bernadette arrived. We went to the hospital together. She decided GP ought to have a nurse & be brought home w. nurses to look after him. We got him a nurse. He looks better. He'll have to stay longer in the hospital though. But his coming home looks possible in a week. B amazed me in her ability to get things done.

The kittens are starting to crawl around in their behind-the-paintings space.

Yesterday I had to go to UE's agency for jobs. It took 15 minutes. They stamped the book & said come back Dec. 7.

My work is not going on . . . drawings that got nowhere. The box is a dead end. I think I need new stuff to work with. Yesterday I drew flowers. Today too. Yesterday I folded some papers & rollered some paint on them. It looks OK but it's nowhere to go. Man . . . do I need ideas. Worse than I need a lover.

Sunday July 18

THIS LONELY LIFE. There's just a veneer of peace & real turmoil underneath.

I feel real urges to purify myself. AGAIN. The last few months have been an indulgence in low poisons. Less pure food—cookies, English muffins on Tuesdays (which I'll still do, I think) cigarettes, coffee. No cigarettes today. I'm lighting every end in sight but soon they'll be finished. I still need coffee to move my bowels. My next shopping trip will be to Greenberg's. Tomorrow I'm going to call and see if I'm eligible for FOOD STAMPS.

I feel good that I've been able to do the yoga exercises. It's about 3 weeks I've been playing with them & since Tuesday I've done them daily. I can't enjoy walking around outside like I did last year. It seems exhausting plus I hate having to put on "street clothes" & pass all those stares. The sun, too, seems so hot.

Last week I had a cheeseburger which made me feel terrible. It was the Tues. after I'd been up til 4:30 at the Emergency Room with GP. Then UE & the hospital again. Then I went to John's. We had some coke & then ate it. I felt so heavy it was really hard to walk. Then I made stroganoff this morn. I liked the sauce but really didn't like eating the meat.

Yesterday I bought & read The Teachings of Don Juan: A Yagui Way of Knowledge. I got stoned—in a good very high way—reading it.

MY WORK seems really stopped. Tues. I'll get more material from H. But I don't feel enthused at all. I feel what I'm doing isn't good enough to be important—That's maybe what's wrong. That I want it to be important so that I'll be famous.

I feel really vacant of ideas. Wait. I know I've been through this before. Is it any different this time?

I keep wanting changes in my whole way of life. A different place to live. Different things to do. NY seems really horrid.

MEETINGS have been getting more imp. to me. I still don't know what I expect from them except to learn abt. me & how I'm dif. fr. & like other women. But that's something. Part of their getting better is bec. they're something to do in an empty time. But also just trying hard abt. anything makes the time you do it better than the rest.

TIME seems very long to me. A week ago seems forever. Bec. of little to do?

Yesterday H talked abt. the CHAKRAS whc. she said were energy-centered—There's one for the self, then sex, then being frugal, then other people, & compassion. I def. feel I went through the sex one last winter & spring 69–70 & I've had to be frugal for so long now. And now sex is a matter not of sex but of other people & feelings. So what's going on? I need some people to be totally involved w.—sexually as well as otherwise—while now it's just otherwise. And they're good relationships but I want a fuller one.

In DON JUAN—which is a very important book—FEAR CLARITY POWER OLD AGE the enemies of the man who wants to become wise. CLARITY was fr... Xmas 69 til maybe Xmas 70. Since then things have become precarious again. Certainly I don't feel power though maybe I did this spring about my work—I don't feel it now.

When I got to D's house I went thru a real withdrawal... I felt awkward being w. them so I just shut up. The acid brought me back—literally & back to fully being in the world.

It's funny I haven't written abt. the acid trip. It was really good. Feeling fine & open & not in need of defenses.

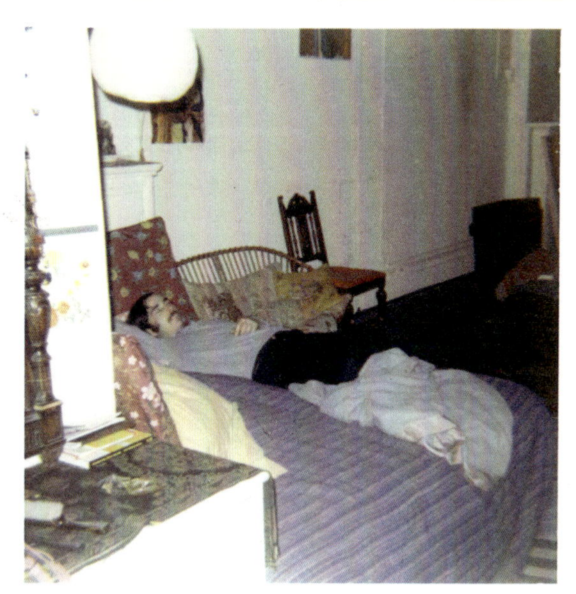

TUES. NOON [July 20]

Yesterday & today have been good. It seems as though my energy is back.

Yesterday I had to go to the hospital & I had decided to go to MOMA to see the Pier 18 show.[29] When I got up I really didn't want to go outside. I hadn't been outside for 2 days. But I went & had the energy to do it without it all seeming like a great effort.

The Pier 18 show seemed like a lot of slightworks. I went upstairs and looked at drawings. I thought about all the kinds of art—drawings—watercolors—that I don't do... I sort of liked Bill Beckley playing the trumpet to his turtle. I didn't want to do yoga yesterday. I bought cigarettes—smoked only a few until the meeting.

At the meeting there was wine & I drank a lot. But I strangely feel OK today. In fact I feel full of energy. And I shat twice—which is a sign of the body working again. Yesterday I didn't do yoga. I didn't want to in the AM & then I was busy. I wish I would want to do it all the time.

At the meeting we talked abt. our relations w. men—sex rel. & what else those rel. entailed. We didn't talk much abt. sex—mostly hist. of how we got involved with people & why we broke up—how our hopes & expectations have changed.

Thurs. we'll have another meeting—where we'll talk abt. just sex.

The meetings haven't changed me—exc. that they've made me feel

29 This exhibition, organized by Willoughby Sharp, consisted of documentation of various artists' projects that took place earlier that year at Pier 18, an abandoned pier on the west side of Manhattan.

good abt. the group & trust the people in it. I learned about B—and I realized that I never trusted my parents—I disc. last night that I've had more relationships than anyone in the group and that I've prob. got more hope for future ones. More than Adrian & Donna anyway.

Thursday 11AM [July 22]

Woke up to the phone Dan Quindazzi wondering if I had his $. Funny how unexcited I was—He makes things sound so prosaic—Europe & his life... He said he'll call next week—I bet not—I wonder would it be different if I saw him—I ought to fall in love with him & we'd live together in a nice loft somewhere.

I couldn't sleep last nite—after I was so tired—it might have been 4:30 or 5—I kept designing houses—how I would arrange things if I had this whole building or Jack's loft—or B's—It annoys me when I do that—it seems like such a waste of time.

Still thinking about drawings... how to deal with detail. Last night I thought of doing a grotesquerie of horrible faces peering out windows—seen through a window with plants on shelves. I'd like to do some art that was arty in the old sense of skillful—& small.

Fri. Midnite [July 23]

Drunk a little again—so many people

Last nite the meeting...the connection of sex & death...how physical affection starts with parents...so their deaths are connected to the next physical affection...and you can't tell people about it... you decide not to & feel cut off...until you overcome the burden... which I haven't done

Yesterday I got more materials from H. I was dragging myself around & only pulled together at the meeting.

Sunday July 25 2:30 PM

Vito called, gotten back from Toronto that morning. He seemed full of energy. He did 8 pieces there in a week. His energy to do work is amazing. He has 3 galleries to decide among for next year. I can tell he is enjoying that position. Such a strange person... I was flattered he called me so soon after returning... Our ties w. each other now are completely our own since they are against every convention. I'm not even that interested in his work as art... much more how it is an expression of him... & how it seems the more he does the more he becomes himself... while he never really changes... his orientation to punish himself carries through.

John came over for dinner. But it seems our relationship is in a low period. Not that I don't want to see him. I really enjoy how we understand each other & can laugh together. Maybe it's just that I feel less sparkly when the possibility of sex is gone. He told me he's been seeing imaginary catastrophes... accidents, fires, collapsing buildings—when he's outside. We dec. it could be caused by a sensitivity to the violent aura of NY. But I'm not satisfied w. that as the only reason. Something else must be stirring him up.

We watched the Soft Skin on TV. I really like it—every time. Prep for Monday's Jealousy meeting. The wife in Soft Skin seems to act out of some blind urge.

Thurs. nite A talked of how she has a schedule for herself—to organize time. So I decided to make one—at least the YOGA, Breakfast, Book, Cleaning part will prob. work—& be helpful—except on Tues. when it will start after UE & a nap.

Tues. July 27

I feel really weak & depressed.

Yesterday Grace & I went to WNYNJ to swim in Jeremy's apt's pool.[30] But the sun never came out. Then we went back to her place for a meeting. Jealousy. It didn't turn me on as last Thursday's did. I was getting tireder all day... I couldn't think by 10:30. Is it that rotten tooth that's acting up?

John called about cats. Cats seem to be taking over my life. Boycat has a girlfriend. A sort of mangy 3-colored creature who has however a lovely bushy tail. I let her in one night & they fought. I've been feeding her bec. she comes to the window and begs... The kittens are getting bigger... I moved them to the cedar trunk so they can walk around—they go all over the place if I let them out... but I felt they should be outside to learn how to run & jump. They walk pretty well by now—they scratch & fight. I just put them out on the loft floor. I hate that they'll get dirty... Then there's feeding Donna's cats every day.

I've washed my hair, made some coffee & opened the curtains. I feel a little better. Saturn is being allowed to crawl around on the desk. He's the most adventurous of the 3—& the smallest. He doesn't seem to like it up here. Rhoda neither. I'll have to be careful not to step on them.

Tomorrow I'll do the laundry. Clean clothes cheer me up. I need a new pair of pants. That I can move in.

30 Rosemary is referring to the town of West New York, New Jersey. Grace Murphy was a friend who attended high school with Rosemary and was also in the consciousness-raising group.

It makes me happy to see the kittens crawling around—I feel as though I'd created them...

Sun. nite I thought of making transparent sacks filled with periwinkle shells. Now I'm thinking about it.

Cleaning on Fri. & Sun. made me feel better about this place.

Today I feel cut off from the world. Make phone calls.

I'll probably read all night. But I want to look at the new materials first... Beginnings of work again...

Yesterday the humidity was unbearable. It's still here today thoughtless. Part of my problems.

I finished A Nin's diary today. She was too good. There's no sex. She never talks about what she does for $... Next I'll read its introduction & then a book abt. traveling in Peru. Tons of books I want to read...

Wed. 11AM [July 28]

A better day. Clear & dry. Makes me happy.

Did yoga & got very tired. Yesterday I tried to learn the Sun Salutation. It's jerky but it's good. Teeth hurt last night 1750 mg of Vitamin C—more later. I cleared a wall yesterday.

12:30 PM

A Nin's Diary makes a different attempt than mine. I try to include everything that's happening to me. Physical, food, exercise she doesn't include. Or the weather & how it affects her—or sex though it's prob. just cut out.

I feel so much more solid & rooted in necessity than she seems to.

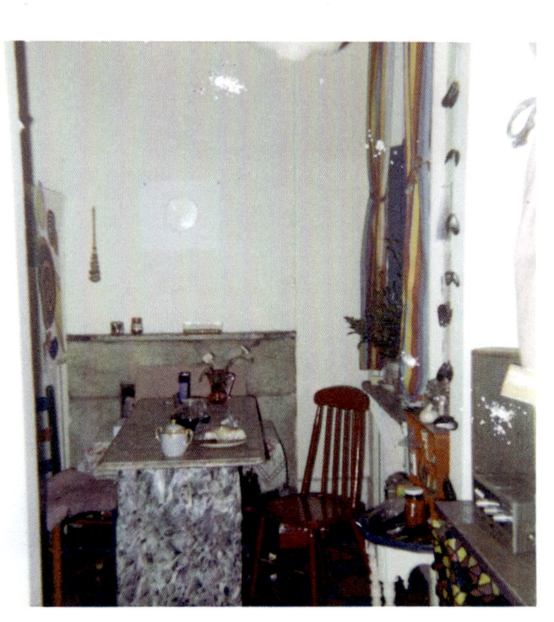

Sunday 3 p.m. [August 1]

FASTING DAY. FEELING HUGE THOUGH 143 THESE LAST DAYS. DAMPNESS SINCE FRI. AND RAIN.

Happy August. I don't really feel happy. Or really bad. Just nowhere. I know I can continue as I am but I want something else. I want ideas & the energy to do them. But I feel so caught here...by small space & dirty walls & floors—

Wed. B & I went to the hospital about 5—GP looked OK but we couldn't make ourselves stay past 10 minutes. GP's sucking my energy dry, mulling my feelings, breaking up my thoughts.

That night at Randa's I enjoyed myself.[31] R, Beth, Grace, Freya & I played w. motion possibilities in a group. We did a lot of touching. I felt rejuvenated. I'd love to live w. a group & do that sort of thing daily. Why do I have so much trouble making myself do yoga in the morning? It ought to be a good way to wake up.

Thurs. AM I paid my bills & went to the NYU Dental Clinic. They said I needed root canals (as always) and put in some temporary fillings (as usual) but my teeth have stopped hurting. Then I went to John's to wait until we could get Adrian & go see Russ Meyer's The Seven Minutes. The movie was just OK—a pretty boring idea of slicing with pornography a story abt. the evils of censorship. But the little tidbits of sex & flesh in jolly Russ Meyer style really turned me on. Giant people—all beautiful—colors & bodies. What a state to bring John home to dinner in.

31 Randa Haines, also referred to as "R," was a regular member of the consciousness-raising group and later became a film director.

Wed. [August 11]

Another hot day. Dristan & moon rising. I would love to be able to record what these days are like. Not bec. I enjoy them, mostly I don't, but bec. they have such a flavor—such a strong feeling...

I wake up first at 7:30 or 8:15. I hear the trucks so I put on the fan. It's already hot & I'm perspiring as I look at the clock & remember it was 3 or 3:30 when I went to bed so I can sleep some more. I have long dreams that are interrupted by flies tickling me, mother cat nuzzling, kittens jumping around the bed. Once or twice a really loud truck will wake me up. I'll rub mother cat's stomach as I return to my dream. This AM I dreamt an end of civilization bec. of a bomb dream. V & K were in it & Dennis & Phyllis. We kept running out of things & figuring out substitutes. Then we dec. all the women had to keep having babies. At eleven was pretty much awake, realizing how hot it was, & wishing I was asleep when St. Joachim called abt. some form the Nursing Home needs. After that I lay back thinking abt. what would be the position of women if the world needed lots of babies. I was rubbing mother cat & thinking too of what shopping I had to do when the phone rang again. It was B who called bec. she's not coming in this week. So if I want to go up there it's 2 fares plus they are busy all day so I'd be stuck at their house. I began to resent the inertia that makes me think it would be best to stay here. Esp. as $ is so tight.

I got up sneezing & realized I had to call Ridgewood. I dragged myself to the bathroom, weighed in at 143, washed my face, brushed my teeth, considered a shower but the water stopped (yest. I took 2—I'll wash away). I fed the cats after sweeping up the dead roaches I'd sprayed last night & rinsing the floor. I realized I was very hungry. I took one Dristan & started some eggs boiling & put on water for coffee. I felt hot, dull & slow. I thought I might feel better if I dressed. While I put on shorts & a blouse & brushed my hair I dec. I needed cat litter & toilet paper. But also some protein. 2 dif. stores are too much especially when one is 15 blocks away. So it would have to be some supermarket impure protein bec. the others are real necessities. I was still sneezing & blowing my nose so w. my vitamins I took another Dristan. Almost immediately, just looking at the coffee, I had to go & shit. The last of the T paper. I thought abt. the drawings I want to do.

And how I'll have to do yoga around 5, shower & eat to get to Randa's at 7:30. Back to the kitchen to eat. A feeling of nausea after I'd finished the grapefruit & was almost finished the eggs. I ate them anyway. I called Ridgewood. I thought abt. calling Vito to get my stapler back—but it's too hot for either one of us to walk to the other's place. I dec. to write in the book, this book. I got matches to light a cigar, brought over an ash tray & the coffee & sat down to this.

Thurs. early morning [August 12]

The drawings are done. They're prob. too little. V was over late last nite & said how they ought to be drawn in colored lines as big as the pieces—on the opp. wall—Since my pieces are def. wall things. I like the idea bec. it would take care of making a viewer think of the convolutions between flat & hung—would get at WALL importance & would at same time present a dif. possibility—depth illusion so that the place of understanding the piece would be only in the viewer's head—not in piece which would look dif. bec. of curves or in the drawing would look dif. bec. of depth illusion. At same time as flat plane of piece is being demonstrated—on flat surfaces—walls, it's being destroyed by gravity & depth illusion.

Thurs.–Fri.–2AM August 12–13

Aug. 12 used to be one of V & my days. Our second date. I think we saw Sons & Lovers. We dec. to get married.

I read a Simenon—Account Unsettled abt. a creepy guy who only wanted food warmth & safety. It was really weird. Now I feel like hiding in my bed for an interminable night.

UE stuff has me freaked again. But I have such good feelings abt. my work. If only I could do it undisturbed by $ worries. What artist hasn't wanted that. If I get a job so UE leaves me alone—I'll be tired & without time.

Since my daydreams of living with Donna—it's strange... I think I only had them as a followup to deciding I could only get out of here by living w. someone. Now that there's even a glimmer of that possibility—I want to continue alone & as free as I am w. my privacy.

I love the night...

Monday Noon [August 16]

All day Sat. I didn't do anything constructive, nec., or esp. interesting. I read a Frank Herbert. I watched TV. I rang D's phone. I talked to A.

I have a lot of trouble relaxing, doing nothing & staying amused. I guess it's fr. always working & having my work & reading to do…so I prob. felt I had no time to waste…and now that I do, I don't know what to do w. it.

A & I spoke abt. my difficulty getting into doing yoga. She said it's bec. I can't get into the present. That's a good description of what's been wrong for the last 7–8 months. Before that I was always enjoying what I was doing bec. I wasn't thinking abt. "what next"…I think several things contrib. to my future itch: thinking abt. getting into a gallery & worrying abt. work & what to do next…wanting to move…all the time in the last months when I've wanted a lover… being on UE & never knowing for how long.

Abt. UE…it makes me think abt. security…makes me think of getting a job & living straight…no art…just money & a clean place to live…whc. would be a real cop out, besides being boring…it's incredible to think that UE can have such a strong influence as to make me think that way.

I'm so pleased to be working again. Another idea yest. for no. 4 in this batch. I wonder when I'll get to it. M is coming over today and then there's the meeting. UE will wreck me tom. Maybe tom. night…or Weds…

D & I went to NJ yesterday to swim & get the sun…Then we came back & had a pizza & talked…

Before we left yesterday she came over here & saw #3 which she liked …D said almost nothing Fri. nite which deadened me a bit…I wish I could get into her work more…but I feel like I did about the box… anything's as good as anything else…her work is so much a part of her subconscious…how can one think or talk abt. it?…

There's a guy in her bldg. who knows abt. some lofts in Bklyn…on Court St for $85 a month…1st glimmer…if only…

This week I should call C Curtis. UGH. But I should.

It's cool, clear & exhilarating today…I wish I could just work on the piece…

Sat. 10:30 AM [August 21]

Yesterday I got a tooth pulled. Thurs. nite I took so many aspirin my ears rang. I couldn't afford a root canal or to wait for NYU's clinic to open in mid-Sept. I saw the dentist at noon. I slept til 8—ate & tried to sleep again abt. 11:30. I felt so terrible I cried. Finally I went to sleep.

UE was uneventful. I flirted with the clerk & escaped. Wed. I went to Ridgewood where all is at least under control & looks better. GP seems to have gained some weight. Then by bus along the old El route—through slums really bad ones to Mary's. Bklyn Heights is such a clean quiet airy relief. She had a slide viewer I wanted & my purple skirt. I bought a pair of size 15 dungarees—plenty of room—I had to take them in at the top but it's nice to have loose pants. Wed. nite V delivered the date for a horoscope I'll do for one of K's school kids—a prize. HOROSCOPES SHOULDN'T BE PARLOUR GAMES.

Thurs. I cleaned the front 2/3 of the floor in the big room—taking aspirin all the while. It got worse. Today I hope I'll have the energy to finish the back of this room. Also need some food. The empty space still hurts.

Monday Aug. 23 10:30 AM

Sat. I cleaned the rest of the house. A clean house really improves my spirits. Less black feet. Sat. was miserable hot. I slept after cleaning & then defrosted the refrigerator. There was so much ice in there I was afraid the thing would collapse supporting it. Then I went over to Vito's to help him w. some photographs—gluing on labels. Kathy came home fr. Southold on LI where she'd been w. her family. V went out for food & we talked. Very depressing conversation abt. how the more you go thru the less fragile & delicate & perhaps she meant sensitive you become. Left so down. Sun. I was telling Donna abt. the talk & she said read Germaine Greer—it all makes you deeper—you only lose the depersonalizing silliness that is still considered by the MCPs to be feminine.[32]

32 MCP was an abbreviation for male chauvinist pig.

Tuesday 7PM Aug. 24

I went back to the dentist. I have an infection & have to take penicillin, not smoke, & drink gallons. I slept all afternoon. It's better to know why I've been feeling so horrible—as though I couldn't react, missed things, had a hundred masks & walls between me & what I did & what I would have liked to have done. Especially with D.

UE was uneventful. I ate a Calzone for lunch...an Eng. Muffin for breakfast & just now some cream cheese. I want to be taken out for Scotches & cheeseburgers. Instead it will be beans & eggs—and beer.

John says Saturn is sucking on Boy Cat's stomach...He seems a little upset at what he called perversion.

I started Back by Henry Green. It's nice. Also the The Four-Gated City by D Lessing which is sociological but bad literature.

7:30 Phillip called...wants to see me...

Wed. August 25

Wedding Anniversary—9 years ago—WOW. That anything could be that long ago…

On my foggy mind…Phillip, Donna, Art…Not bad topics…Last night I did some drawings of impossible knotted sewed & twisted pieces. But very rough drawings which I think today I will do over more finely.[33] Finally something that makes sense to draw…bec. it couldn't exist any other way.

C Curtis finally called…not until Sept.

33 These are the drawings shown on pages 123–127.

Drawings, August 1971

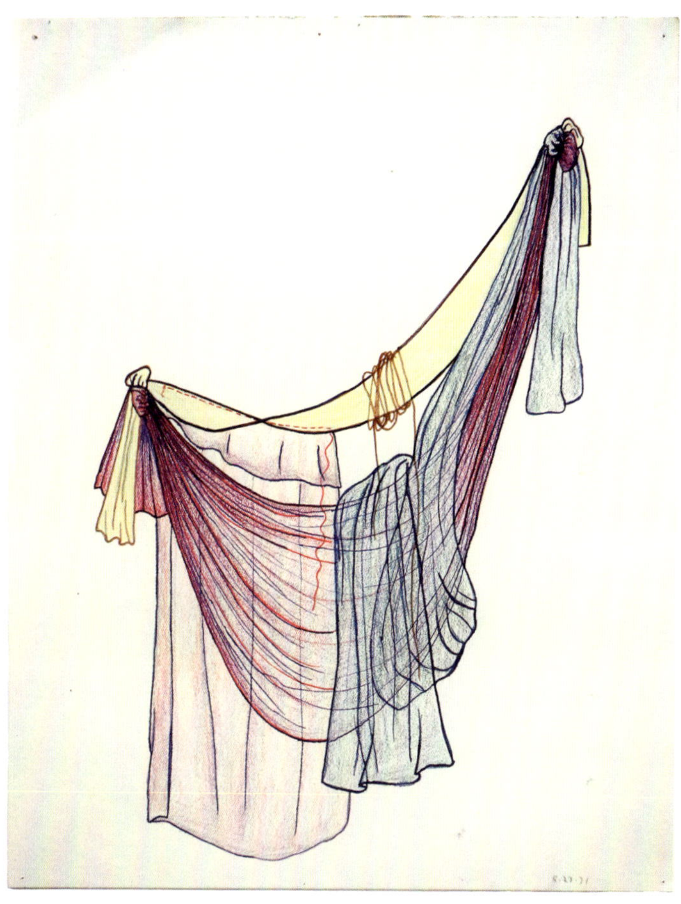

Untitled, 8.23.71. Colored pencil and colored marker on paper, 12 × 9 in.

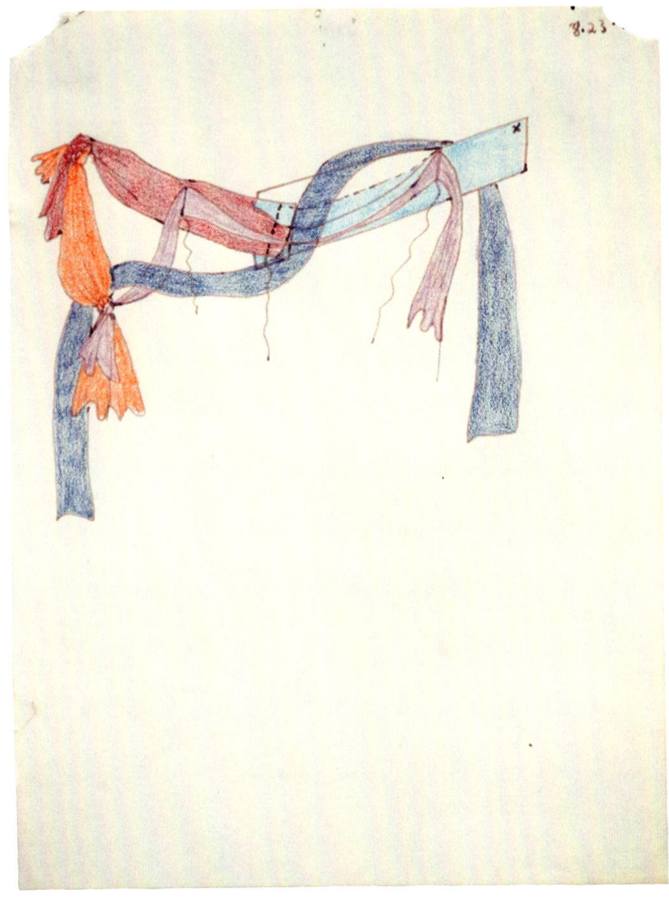

Untitled, 8.23.71. Colored pencil and colored marker on paper, 12 × 9 in.

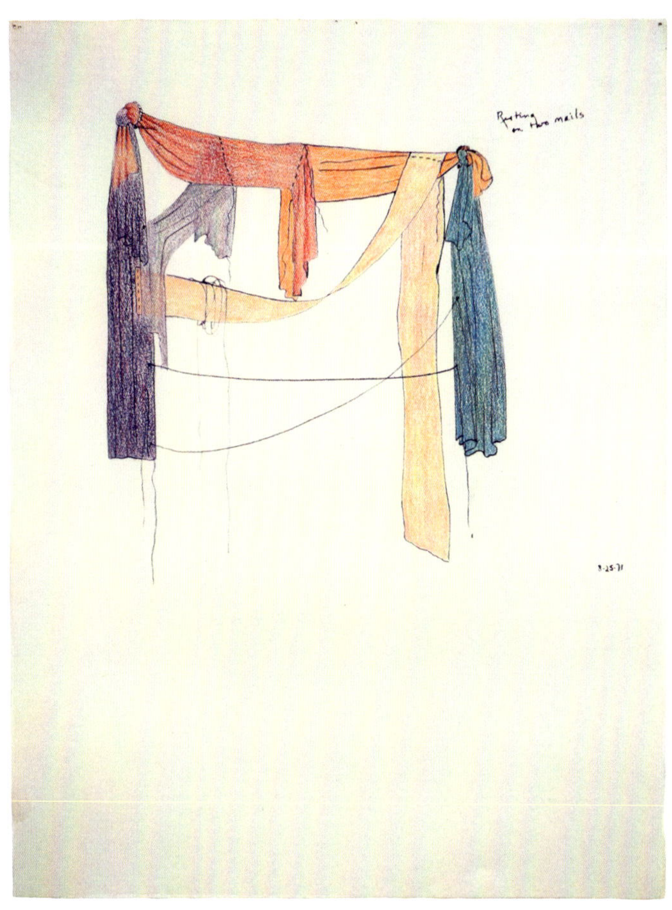

Untitled, 8.25.71. Colored pencil and colored marker on paper, 12 × 9 in.

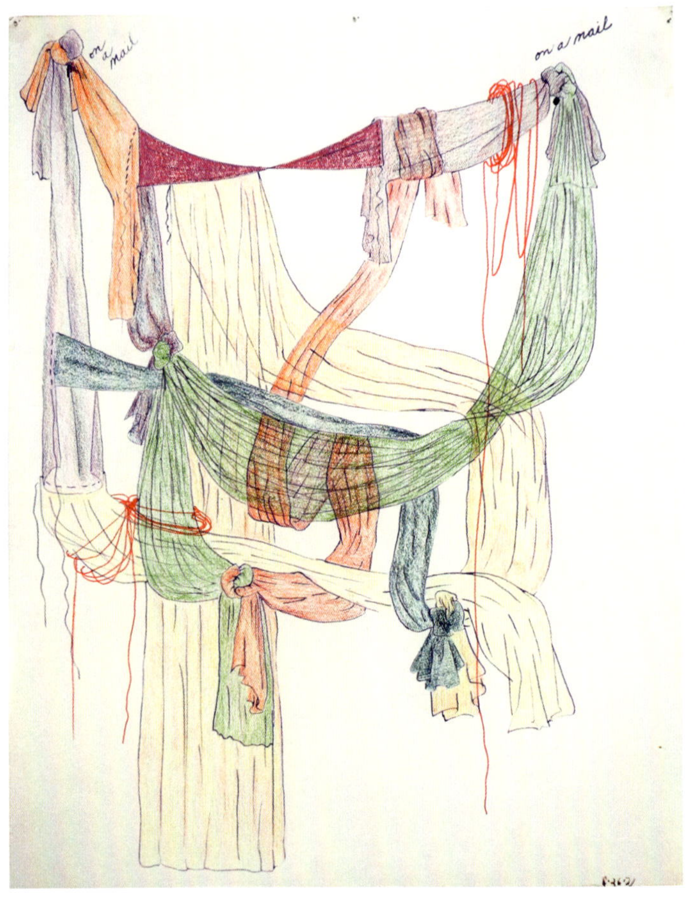

Untitled, 8.26.71. Colored pencil and colored marker on paper, 12 × 9 in.

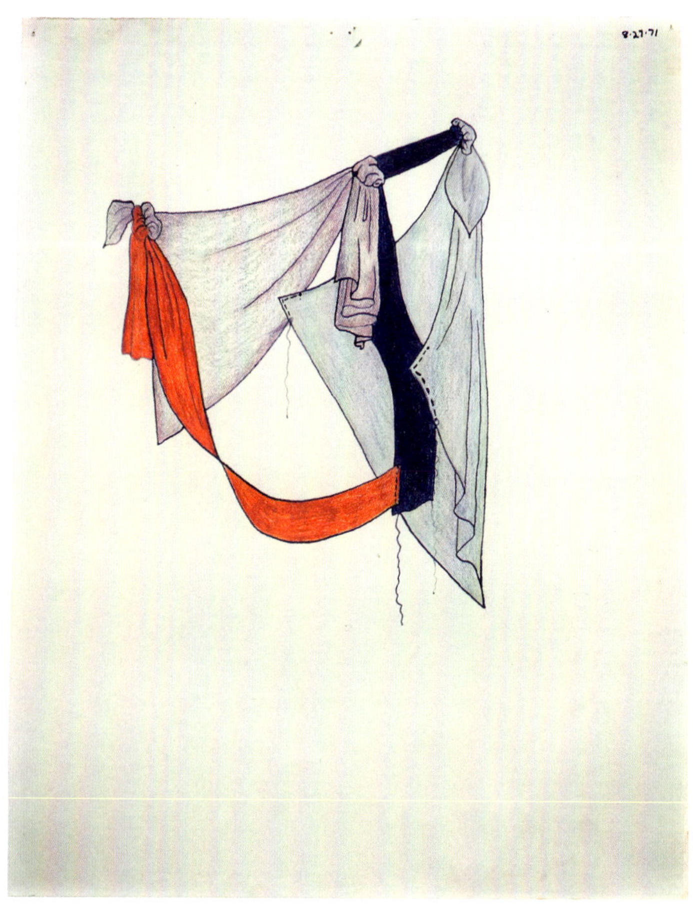

Untitled, 8.27.71. Colored pencil and colored marker on paper, 12 × 9 in.

Fri. 1 PM Aug. 27

A pouring rain day.

It had better stop raining so hard. The roof upstairs is leaking & so is the upstairs fireplace. Muddy water has started coming through my fireplace... 2 of my nice jars are sacrificed to catching leaks in the upstairs fireplace. Would it do any good to complain... I hate those guys so.

Last nite the woman's march.[34] Very straight & concerned w. getting into politics. No euphoria just lots of women.

I've been making a lot of drawings—of impossible pieces—I like them bec. it's a chance to play w. colors & all the possibilities of draping, tying, sewing, etc...w. o. $ & they can be unfettered by space & size...what they do is actualize in real materials—paintings—relations of colors & shapes & space. Donna said they were Baroque...whc. is true—they are complex & dramatic. I like them but they seem not to go far enough... I think I'll make some simpler ones whc. show a few things more clearly...though simpler ones go against my nature whc. is Baroque I think...last night we looked at Colin Greenly's work... glassy plastic crystal things—man-size decorations...are mine very different? Mine are more concerned w. the stuff they use...their forms come from what materials do...& what I can do to them...there's color too...

34 This was the second women's liberation march in New York to mark the anniversary of women's suffrage and protest inequality.

Tuesday August 31, 11 AM

The last few days my head has become very unclear... I've felt like marshmallows & mashed potatoes in mind & body. I'm up to 144... period coming. I have no urges to do any particular work but I feel I ought to be doing work w. all this time. The materials I have left don't appeal to me... they seem small & uninterestingly colored...

A was here last nite & gave her usual put down of the work... that it was all too tasteful & not new enough... From what she says I ought to quit... and it would be better to make deliberately ugly pieces without new ideas than these... I do think these pieces are full of new ideas... as for their being tasteful... I think they're on the edge... the pastel ones on the edge of ugliness... the other jarring in their color combinations.

A & D last nite suggested graduate school & teaching... and grants. I think I will apply for a Guggenheim... & the Council on the Arts... get Vito & Sol to write recommendations...[35]

Described Simenon's Account Unsettled to V this AM & got excited abt. it again.

Took Farouk to be deballed this AM. Terrible. The movies w. J tonite?? UE uneventful. Tom. model.

35 The artist Sol LeWitt, whom Rosemary knew through Adrian Piper. LeWitt and Piper lived in the same loft building on Hester Street.

Sun. noon Sept. 5

The application scares me bec. it asks for "position" & shows. All day yest. horrible hay fever. D was here to sew. We spent the whole day tog. I went over to her place afterwards—abt. 7 to avoid being here alone & feeling horrible. She cleaned her house & I read. Then she made a cheese omelet w. some cream. Yummy. Around 11 I came back & watched a movie, read the paper & slept til 10:45. 8 hours 45 min.

Fri. nite I made a piece w. a pair of pants & a shirt some horrible pastel scraps... I don't like it today bec. the scraps are all that pastel underwear color & small too... M I spoke to this AM says she'll bring me some material she doesn't like.

I wish I had lots of fabric & could do some work today. Everything that's left is hopeless... more drawings? I feel too much like doing something big... but maybe it should be drawings.

Yest. would have been a terrible day w. o. D.

Tomorrow modeling at 10 & a meeting at nite. That leaves me the afternoon. Tues. UE—Wed. & Fri. I will model I hope... The rest of the time??? sort of scares me... why?... bec. I want to accomplish something great & I'm afraid I won't & will settle for reading & cleaning & eating & sleeping...

Tues. nite: Meeting me & D specific, A, B, G—idealistic & enraging.

Thurs. 4 PM, Sept. 9

I've been in a strange frame of mind or really strange frames of mind... not at all articulate abt. feeling either. More bad dreams... of amputation this time. All of a sudden mosquitoes and loneliness & horniness. D's gone to Denver. I miss her already. Right now I feel good. I've been drinking dandelion tea, calamus tea which is supposed to curb your desire for tobacco, ate a grapefruit & a dandelion salad & did yoga & bathed. I feel nice. Maybe I can write everything out, though I'm very restless...

This weekend I tried to cut down on cigars & to eat better. I managed to do yoga too... & Mon. I felt pretty good. I modeled & went to the park. There was a meeting that nite which left me unsatisfied. G & B went off to eat afterward & I was hurt they didn't ask me.

I feel like jumping out of my skin...

Tues. UE was nothing. Then house chores & a movie, Don Siegel's The Beguiled, which I liked & has stayed in my mind. The natural lighting, the covered-over evil, revenge, etc. in all the characters. Pretty good. I was really turned on & flirted w. all the clerks in GB's afterwards & enjoyed walking back w. John. But once back here... a nap & then helping D w. her dress for the Denver wedding. She being lucid & vindictive & prob. justly vindictive abt. G, B, & A's idealism...

Yesterday I modeled & ran around getting anti-mosquito things. Then M called & took me to the Wild Mushrooms for dinner. She was in high spirits so it was a pleasure. Sleep at 12:30 until 9 or so & then I lolled in bed till 10:45... and had some bad dreams.

2 days ago seems forever ago. Today I went to get grapefruit, talked on the phone, etc. as above. Many feast preparations outside. Maybe that energy is affecting me. I finished Don Juan II...great book...I want more...

I want to do work but I don't know what to do. I'm not in the mood for more drawings...maybe tonight when it's dark...I wish I had more materials...Maybe I should make drawings of the possibilities w. what I have...all on one page...DO IT...tonite.

Sun. Noon Sept. 12

Inarticulate Days. I got nicely stoned last nite w. J & D. I wished for another life. I know how to live this one & even be happy in it. I wish I had a way to make $. I'll prob. go to Mass.

Thurs. & Fri. I finished a piece & started another. Thurs. nite H called & invited me to Woodstock. Cats & $. Fri. modeled, slept, went to Vito's piece at WS's—threatening anyone who would try to come into his cellar.[36] Nice. I never got the $3 for advertising their cat. They're off to Nova Scotia. B unfriendly again that nite. Home to finish piece. Watched Lost Horizons.

Sat slept late. Fed D's cats. Bought cigars. Rain. Worked on new piece. Went to J's for fish dinner. Walking in the sick yellow rain on 23rd Street. Watched Brothers Karamazov.

Many dreams... all these days.

36 This is Acconci's video, *Claim Excerpts*. "WS" is likely Willoughby Sharp.

Thurs. Sept. 23

The country was pleasant, green & clean as always. Casey & Kathe are becoming so American small town...but I suppose as long as they do it consciously it's fine. I could never. As always I hated coming back to dirt & murk & smoke & grit...and also to being alone after 6 days of constant company. That feeling at least is gone & I'm OK here alone.

Yesterday I did the Guggenheim application writing. Now I need a typewriter. Then I went to John's & learned how to play chess. D is living there. It makes me sad though I like her. She has bought one of those lovely coats w. leg of mutton sleeves fr. Countdown. How I wanted her life w. J...and her coat. I am always left to myself...

When I came back I looked at the last piece I'd finished before I left & thought it cute, too little in scale, doing nothing w. color. Soooo...

I called Curtis who again put me off.

I called H in Woodstock & we had a long talk...about Chakras bec. in Mass on mescaline I saw stars of light coming out of my body at points along the lines of the chakras—up to my forehead...I wonder if things are so separated & ordered as this part is this, the next that...We also talked abt. art...my continuing to do it...my going to Woodstock for the winter with H. What do to w. this place if I did... if I'd like living w. H...

I feel like making pieces isn't that impt. Now...the ideas I've been using I've had for a while...so the pieces don't really turn me around...Soooo...

I need to think of birthday presents for M & A...a present for C & K...

Sunday 6:20 PM Oct. 3, 1971

I want something I don't have. I'm not as satisfied as I was in the time I now remember so fondly—winter 69—spring & summer 70. After Maine in Aug. 70—itchiness of dissatisfaction—wanting—a show & then around Xmas—my birthday wanting love—a want which hasn't been satisfied yet—10 months—now since my wanting a new place to live—in short wanting a whole dif. life...

I haven't done yoga much since Mass.—& no work—a lot of people & aimlessness—modeling

Women's meetings—strength fr. something to do.

Pass hours with John or Donna on the telephone. No trees and dirty feet.

Last nite & made dinner for J & D & D—not especially good food or conversation but I feel good about it—I have a hangover but I feel cleaned out & energized—

I really enjoyed dressing up last night...I wish I were an elegant lady of 1880—clean & beautiful a <u>thing</u> to look at w. pleasure...to bask in admiration.

What have I done?

Tues.—meeting—galleries in the afternoon

Wed.—modeled—tired walked in the park

Thurs.—modeled, preg. test & John's

Fri.—modeled, looked for a loft around East Broadway

Sat.—cooked, saw D, dinner

Today—late breakfast w. D—here for a TV movie—waiting to hear fr. Mary—

Phillip's been calling—I don't know what to say to him. I want someone to love but it's not him.

Sat. Oct. 9 6PM

Nothing seems right... no words of description abt. how I feel... nothing that I feel or think... which is practically nothing at all—

How have I frittered away another week...?

Mon. I modeled, as I did all week, got my glasses fixed, saw the Conformist, bought SF books & a Joan Didion (UGH)

Tues.—UE Modeling... Grace's and a meeting...

Wed.—Modeling & John to the galleries, then the play B & E worked on.

Thurs. Modeling, chess, typing CAPS application.[37]

Fri. Modeling & GBs for vitamins & a little food.

Today too I modeled & went to get A's horoscope—brought the application to D...

I looked at my chart. It's a month since I did any work... and I don't know what to do either...[38]

All week I have been reading SF & detective novels. Today I read Raphael's book of remembrances...

I feel vague... drifting ...what's going on... dim thoughts of drawing flowers, these rooms...

37 This refers to the Creative Artists Public Service, a grant program of the New York State Council on the Arts. Rosemary received a grant from them in 1977.

38 This may be an example of Rosemary being hard on herself, as during the past month she did work on some new pieces as well as grant applications.

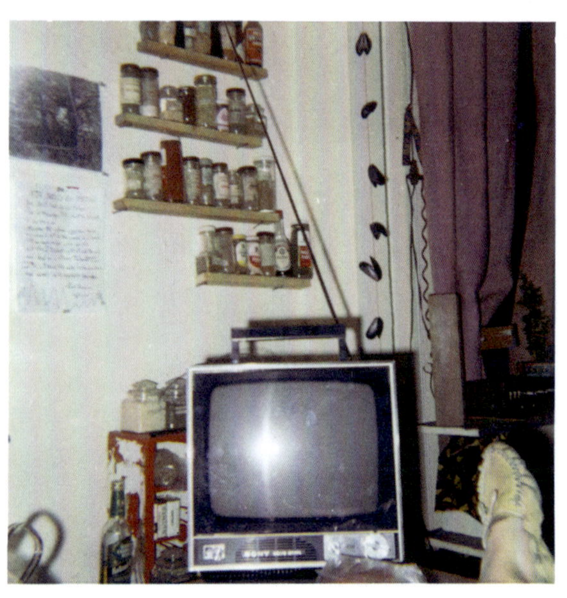

How dif. R's life was fr. mine...

The cats are so friendly—not to each other—to me...

I've been very tired the last few days—6 ½ hours of sleep all week because I've been reading—Ray Bradbury is OK. Delaney stinks. Didion I thought was phoney.

I feel immobilized by this place... unable to find a new one...

So often I've thought how I'd like to be a hundred yrs. ago & just paint ... is R creeping into me?... should I just do it?... paint what? I'm lost...

It's too crowded here... and falling apart...

Sunday nite, Oct. 10, 1971

Everybody has bad days. That's small comfort...none at all...when I've done no work in a month and my mind seems to be blocked...I eat a delicious little purple plum that I drew last night because I could think of nothing else to do...and I wonder if inactivity is making me fat...or if I should even feed myself when I am so useless... I try to comfort myself with all the practical things I've gotten out of the way...glasses fixed, boots repaired, the dentist...Comfort has appeared twice...because this state has no comfort...not for the soul, none for any part...one never really rests because nothing is ever over when nothing is begun...I want to move. I feel as though this place is falling in on me. The peeling paint is a sign for my mind... sifting sand...with nothing in sight...Tomorrow I'll be busy outside... modeling I'll see R working away...I'll think of not knowing what to do...of not being able to affect anything but to keep on living...in this city living has few pleasures...the sun doesn't really shine...I have no lover...I've been smoking again...I'll play chess to absorb myself...then I'll go to the women's meeting...more to see people... I guess I really expect little else from it...I know I can live my life...I know about injustice. Tuesday I'll go to Unemployment hoping they'll leave me alone...then to the dental clinic...Tuesday night, Tuesday afternoon even I'll be wondering what do to with myself... Wednesday I'll model, deliver the hopeless Guggenheim application, pick up Adrian's horoscope...do it...then what...my work is in a jam...I can't find a new place to live...I'm annoyed by the clutter in my closets, old clothes, old records, old jars of paint...the next time I have nothing to do I could throw things away...I always find something to do with them later on...I've read so many books lately...one and two a day...I'm lonely, not horny, lonely. I feel as though I can't do work here anymore...that I have to stop thinking... I'd feel better if I could get going on something. The place wouldn't be the only thing to look at.

I have in the last weeks of not doing any work come to some working hypotheses (plural) about the states of my affairs...

One is that what really turns me on about art, is looking at art, that I love visually arresting, interesting to caress with the eyes art...which only goes along with my sensual nature...please me everything...do it...but looking is really the most important channel for me...

Two is that I am still in love with...

Three is hard to explain...it's that each action, or state, or feeling doesn't have to be definable as one way or the other...I can't really explain it...which is an example of it...that everyday isn't "good" or "bad"...that an unsettled feeling in my stomach isn't a sure sign of something...that I should be able to name and judge...that there's no reason to expect things to work out in some definite way...that things are gray rather than black or white...that expecting the black or the white and waiting for it makes you miss the peculiar gray...it all just goes along...indefinable...

Thurs. Oct. 21 11 PM

This weekend I was sick I guess w. a virus & today I'm dead & achy & feverish again. But my stomach is OK.

I've got an idea for a new piece—an idea brought on by a painting I saw at OK Harris by David Lewallen. Squares of cloth overlaid w. edges hanging out—slashed...

But I've got to do something abt. this place...it's too depressing...

Last night dinner w. Jim Carroll[39]...I liked him & hope we'll see each other again...he has nice curly steel grey hair...though he's not esp. attractive he looks comfortable...When he left he said I wasn't so formidable as I seemed...He mostly listened to me...

I've begun to polish my nails, I wore makeup a few times...Mary's party & to see Rick, to John's & to see Jim. I want clothes.

I hope I have energy tom. to start cleaning up...

A Heineken is making me feel better...

I feel good abt. myself lately—got down to 139 last week but am up to 143 again...but I do feel I look good...I hope JC will call tonite... though I'm already telling myself to calm down

I've still got it for John. But...it's OK too as it is. JC called him my slave...

Rauschenberg's cardboard pieces are good. Tomorrow I promised

39 This Jim Carroll, whom Rosemary also refers to as JC and J Carroll, is not the well-known writer and musician.

after much prodding to bring Raphael my slides…
DUMDEDUMDUM

Whitney today some unimpressive Hoppers…The meetings are getting boring…

Still smoking.

Sunday Oct. 24—4 PM

Last nite J Carroll again. If he keeps on saying stay as long as you like I just might. Dinner & drinking places—3 scotches much wine...

I'm all shaky today...fr. drinking...I can't make myself do any work ...I really didn't want to leave...but I didn't know what to do if I stayed...

I'm already redesigning his house in my head...What if I lived there and rented a studio...the way my work's been going...what if I lived there...

Maybe knowing I have him will enable me to quit smoking...he went out and got me some cigarettes this AM...gave me $10 for a cab...I'll have to give it back to him Tuesday...he's coming for dinner.

He says lovely things...it's funny how I like being really close to him—feeling him alongside me...funny too how he's not especially handsome...just tall & big...w. silver hair...he has nice blue eyes...I loved sleeping curled up with him...I really want to be near him again...thank goodness I've got lots to do until Tues.

Mon. nite [Oct. 25]

Was that apt. a womb—enclosed safe hugged together—if it was... it was still good...but my need for that could get claustrophobic, clinging...I thought I was finished w. all that...real stirrings...not that I want to put down how much I enjoyed us tog....but it just can't be all the time & it's mixed—good love & questionable receding into a totally safe environment.

Today's emotion went from pleasant sadness to anticipation to fear... what's next? This weekend was a lot to live up to...so few times I've wanted time to stop...though that dim nest did seem separate from other reality...that's what was so good and so dangerous at the same time.

Also the similarities bet. us—the I Ching abyss doubled was maybe about 2 super soft people...my eternal fear of floating, dissolving in a miasma of inactivity...is in JC too I think...and so is the sweet softness that accompanies being that disparateness...

Everything seems double edged tonite—

October 30 Sat. 4:45 PM

I really like the new piece…though I don't know what to do to it next. Weds. nite I made 2 drawings of it…whc. I don't like now…but the piece just seems like a jumble/jungle of possibilities though of course I'm worried abt. what to do next…

Abt. JC—effects—went to a clothes store & tried things on. I've painted my nails again. I borrowed shoes from D. I bought new mascara & a new brush (whc. I've been thinking of doing for abt. 8 mos. now)

I spent too much time thinking abt. something to wear—I'm annoyed at myself for that…

But it's fun to think of myself as a decorable thing…& to feel desired…whc. gives a point to the decorating.

I was also thinking of the great pleasure I find in gracefully performing some very old love actions…like rec. flowers…or offering food…of kissing or caressing…on this: 1) it's decadent… though I don't think in any way evil…bec. it is concerned w. forms… not the substance, actuality, of myself or the other person, but concerned w. the elegance in watching or being watched…& doing…the pleasure comes not fr. the action itself but from the stored up associations, images, mostly ones I've read…& from repeating beautifully this ancient pattern…

The danger is that one could easily, when one is me & I'm w. someone else who enjoyed these patterns, not really see the other or enjoy him—just be enjoying the patterns…if one could do both…it would be fine…

But not doing these things... & closing my mind to the multiple pleasures they offer... is like getting dressed carelessly & purposefully looking sloppy... it's a pointless omissive action to convince me & others I'm avant-garde... when really I'm just cutting off a possible source of great pleasure for myself & others...

Also I think my mood is really changing... I think JC has something to do w. it... but it's been a while coming...

Getting sick is a sign of a shakeup too... all connected... I feel freer than ever—& I felt freer than before the last time. I feel more able than ever to live... the change is somehow connected to that thing I realized a few Sundays ago... that things aren't one way or the other... don't have to be clear, right—just are... inviolably

Like the stone steps that never moved when I was a kid... And I can go on better now that I know this... it's hard to explain... everything doesn't have to be optimum... even... like the Greek proverb—one misses a lot looking for the biggest things.

Maybe this is all too proud...

Anyway whatever it is... it's connected to my new way of being able to work without all the actions being set out in my head ahead of time... Another thing—this J Carroll thing has to be kept fr. any semblance of routine... routine anything... sex, food, clothes, places, people... I do feel I'm pulled back a little... bec. of all the phone calls? Thurs. nite... twice last nite... this afternoon... bec. I'm sick... but why does it bother me... I don't feel so romantic either... bec. I'm sick?... though I want to make love... it's great having something happen that gives me all these thoughts... it's what I wanted... and I sure waited long enough...

I feel like 17 again... & no one I don't think has done that to me—
I'm going to be late... but I just can't rush...

Mon. Nov. 1

It's hot & damp & mosquito weather. But my mind is on work & JC Work in that I'm wondering if I'm any good...what I'm doing on this new thing—playing w. boundaries—?? how's that related my past material mindedness ... I'm worried...I loved working today but worry that it was bad work...

Abt. JC—I love to be w. him...but what do I love?...being adored, fed, petted, made love to, companioned...is that fair?...I feel a real sympathy—an intuitive understanding of what he's like & what life is like for him...& I admire his courage to keep on going...not that I mean I think his life is all terrible...but he's like me...the going is thick w. lots of bad & lots of lonely times...& he has the same ability I've dev. to hold onto what present pleasure & joy there is...also he understands things of the spirit...understands understanding...

I must be in a bad & critical mood...I've just written a lot of awfully good things...to be worried...

I'm rankled by Grace being sharp at the meeting, & feeling I was saying a lot of dumb stuff.

Abt. JC too, I'm really attracted to how he looks...

Abt. work...I'd be so much better into it if I could talk to someone who did work like it...R says I need encouragement...it's true...

Abt. JC—his house except for one room...is quite dark...what does that imply...a desire not to see everything as it is—? whc. is understandable though I couldn't not just turn on every light w. 500 watt spots...but it's odd how safe & peaceful I feel there...bec.? I don't have any responsibilities but being me...talking, making

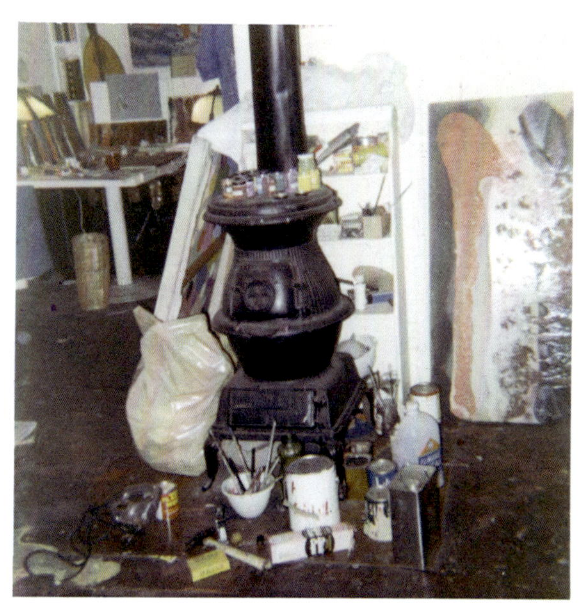

love...he has to feed us, put out the garbage, wash the dishes—be resp. for clean glasses—

It's touching—this weekend all the sheets were clean—the whole place was, the bathroom was full of towels and a bathrobe bec. I said I wanted to take a bath, he'd gotten odd fruit like I had on Tuesday—& nuts...he even thinks I don't eat enough...

Last nite I couldn't get his image out of my mind...

Today I really wanted to work—& I could & did—24 hr. vacations are great as restoratives...out & away fr. this gritty place...into a cleaner, softer one...it's really good for me...But I don't want to be using him...which is why I went through that whole long thing of why I liked him...to be sure there were reasons...or was it to be sure I didn't...I really am freaky tonite.

GO TO SLEEP

Grace called me Gloomy Gus

Nov. 9. Tues.

IN TURMOIL—I'VE DONE IT—THINGS HAVE CONVERGED.

I've been fluctuating bet. happy rapturous love hazes, incredible fear, deadness, worry, making art & losing sense of time. I'm afraid I'm in love w. being in love & not with JC—but I don't want that to be true—that would be to use him as an object...

Last nite I spent w. him—bec. Sun. I had to leave abt 7:30 to go to a meeting... and I didn't want to so arranged to see him Mon. nite... but I was tired... after Sun. meeting D & I ate & drank & talked until 2—then I had to model Mon. & go to CAPS & by 6 I was really tired...

I had wanted to go up there & have a super romantic time... tell him I loved him... do I?... Michael said how he couldn't like J—so I was troubled... how I let things get me... MF is OK but hardly a guide for my life... anyway... I used the keys he gave me Sun... I'd wanted to do that... he was in bed & took time to wake up... everybody does exc. me when I'm w. people... we went to the Ideal Restaurant—stifling place w. sort of grubby but very filling food... he looked great in a blue jacket... we looked in stores... I felt like a little girl... we played chess... & I played very badly, whc. upset me... we watched a little TV—he made plans for a trip to Fishers Island... I felt all the while I was too tired... he was tired... then when I disc. he had to get up at 6:30... I felt like running home... but after I asked should we make love—we did... it was lovely quiet... He said we're not relaxed enough... whc. increased the way I already feel... that I don't know how to do this... be w. him... think abt. it... act... I feel that my super romanticism... rapture... is schoolgirlish... & I don't know how to be but that way or a friend...is this true? It's not quite it but I feel inadequate.

This relationship is going fr. the initial unreal romantic all the time stages into contact w. real life...work, Fishers Island...being tired... so now what will happen...I feel it's an imp. point...to pass it & feel OK would be something I guess I've never done...not w. Vito with whom I had the romantic part & the rest fucked us over...& w. no one else...friendly love for John & though mixed w. romance was always kept cool by J...& practical...in touch w. practical reality bec. he is...

I'm still wanting to build satin & silk tents...filled w. flowers and jasmine smells & languorous love...which ought to be allowed to happen—(decadent? So what)

Today is a white sky winter day when your head has to be fine to beat the bleakness of outside & the grey light.

Last week on the phone Carroll told me he loved me...I hesitated... said wow...or some such nit-wit-ism...& he said "whatever that means"...which I supposed was only healthy face saving...since I hadn't come back w. the same...but I've been wondering—hard— D, A, G, Jane all thought at the meeting I was in love...I did too... until & I couldn't believe it...

Sun. I was so sad to leave him...Tues. sad to have him leave here... Really sad...distraught...unable to do anything...confused...

So what's going on...am I worried bec. he's not an artist...he is so like me...do I want an "important" lover & am I unwilling to be involved w. "just" a nice guy...

I feel like I am beating my head ag. the wall...not getting to the bottom of this . . .

This AM when I left I left notes all over, one that said call me up a lot I'll miss you this weekend—and lots more—persimmons, wine, apple sauce, warmth, the moon, stars & lots more—from R who loves you.

DO I love him? . . .

Well I'll have lots of time to think . . . this weekend he has to go to Boston . . . & I've got to see Casey & Kathe . . .

Other things—A liked the new piece

At the meeting they seemed to think I was jealous of John's Donna.

11 pm Thurs. Nov. 18

Everybody is freaking out...B, Grace, Kathy D...I'm OK...I'm fine ...great...though UE's after me. Being so in in love w. J makes it OK...Work...I want to do drawings of canvas piece but I can't settle down...not Tues...and yesterday when I just wanted Jim...not tonite when I saw D...and drank and drank...but I don't feel bad abt. it...I've worked hard...though sometimes I feel not hard enough...of course...

Holly Solomon...[40]

JIM CARROLL

I LOVE HIM

Sleeping at his house...Love & yogurt at 7AM...writing notes til 9:30 & hopping off to Raphael...

These are good times...

I deserve them...

He does too...

FINE FINE FINE...

40 Holly Solomon was another influential gallerist. Rosemary was preparing for a studio visit with her, as noted in the next entry in which Rosemary refers to her as HS.

Nov. 23 11PM

The writing was clearer at the beg. of the month & in Oct. I'm not sure why lately I've been unable to get into this.

Work—I've been too busy outside—w. UE fake job trips, dentist, CAPS—Today I did a piece w. the 3 pinks some wire whc. is only a statement of ideas of allowing etc. w. whc. I'm now bored... but no new ideas seem to be there. The last rectangles piece hasn't led anywhere. It seems like arty over-knowing doodling. I try to draw the pieces—whc. are all up for HS but have had little time so that's not led anywhere... I don't really think it will... It will just keep my mind on the work while I do it... it's been so long since I was really working. I'm scared but what's to be done? But wait... looking at so many pieces here now—some seem quite good... others not so good... I feel I haven't tried hard enough... gone far enough... but now I don't know where to go... I also feel the work is getting dated ... there's lots of "materials" art around... would I just groan if I saw it in a gallery? I worry that I'll lose myself in JC—not leave enough time for work & thought.

But I've thought some good thoughts bec. of him. The strong feelings I have for him have shown me how shallow were all those silly relationships—Charles esp... but shown it to me better... esp. abt. John... how John & I were so separate in our pleasure... how much more I love Jim... I find nothing to put me off... I feel so close to him it's sort of incredible... Life is better by far... I daydream abt. him instead of dwelling on $ problems, galleries etc... though I fear the extent to whc. he fills my mind maybe takes a little art time thinking away... maybe but I'm not sure bec. I've always had to push my head into constructive art thoughts...

These days I feel I've spent so little time working. I doubt my artist self... its worth & its strength & the extent to whc. it is a part of me...

Jim takes the edge off things... I don't feel really really bad abt. work bec. of the time thing... but I could feel worse w. o. him.

He takes the edge of course off loneliness... knowing we'll be all wrapped up tog. soon makes it pleasant to be here even desperate...

His place takes the edge off this place.

Going out with him takes the edge off poverty...

I worry that he loves me more than I love him... that I'm getting too much... comfort, dinners out that I enjoy & make me less able to just love him...

His generosity is amazing... It far outdoes me when I had money... though it's of that fine sort... his sweetness it sounds corny but he is sweet... He was here tonite & already I'm waiting for Thurs... Thanksgiving... it should be fun... Donna is having an orphan dinner—to whc. I invited Phillip & w. hesitations now that I've done it... but Jim coming down later & I'll enjoy dressing up & then later being w. just him.

Tuesday Nov. 31 11:30 PM

These lovely days. I'm so happy most of the time & full of good memories. Today was a delight. UE was 15 min. and then I went to Macy's w. an envelope full of $80 fr. J who insisted I needed a coat & boots—for weeks I refused the $ but everyone in the group said why not—except A who thinks it's dep. on men—anyway I floated thru Macy's looking for boots & found a fantastic dark blue cape fr. Denmark—it seems warm too & bought it. It made me tremendously happy. Of course I wonder am I a fool to take such pleasure in possessions but then I discount the worry... how often do I get clothes... my long skirt & this... then I went to Bloomingdale's to look for coats. I felt so bubbly I wanted to see someone & called up Donna for a cheap lunch—more boot looking & home to call J.

The weekend was filled w. delights—dressing up for Thanksgiving—I love how I looked—so did J—I'm vain—vain bec. really I doubt how gd. & if I look gd.—so I'm worried & then overly pleased that I do look gd.—I doubt it's a vice in any case—just a weirdness—navy blue blouse over black leotard—long skirt—watch & red stocking w. silver shoes—but I was tired & too drunk—Phillip glared at my turkey eating kept me from eating enough—& I wanted to eat more bec. it was good—so I was in a sort of inactive haze—Jim looked great to me—Linda Schjeldahl was overbearing to J & Phillip—finally we left & went to J's... We both said we were too tired for sex & talked for a long time. He is wise—

Fri. we went looking for boots & found none & I went to see Rosselini's Socrates—which was nice colors & OK & stark—then J cooked his first cheese omelet—he & me—tired talked & decided to sleep early—a nap til 3AM...

Sat. I came home but couldn't do anything & got grumpier—went to the galleries & saw Joan Snyder who wasn't as good as I expected & some nice Nauman perception pieces—I wasn't too happy when I met Jim & Mary for dinner—

that was OK—then J & D came to Jim's & we watched some science movies he'd taken from his school. They were pretty. He is really knowledgeable. We talked abt. scientific things. It was interesting & I kept thinking—not a word abt. art—when they left I said he was tired…

Sun. I didn't know how long he wanted me to stay w. him—we went to the Cloisters to meet Rita a friend of his & then to Port Authority to meet someone else—then we went to the Wild Mushroom & played chess over dinner—then walked through the W. Village & went to Remington's—more chess & back to his house—we sat & looked at each other for an hour maybe—it was lovely…

Model, Sam G at the MOMA, sleep, meeting—and then today—[41]

Thurs. I visited GP Ugh—he didn't say a word to me—

I like my new idea—in a calm sort of way—I feel no rush to do it. I couldn't find the right material in Macy's.

I feel so busy these days—the mornings to Raphael—2 afternoons to NYUD[42]—Tues. are good when UE leaves me alone—Mondays seem to disappear bec. of tiredness & the meetings at nite—but I'm happy.

41 A show of Sam Gilliam's painted and draped canvases, part of a series called *Projects* at the Museum of Modern Art.

42 This is likely New York University's dental school.

Sun. nite Dec. 5 11:30 PM

Fri.—race track w. brother Brian & wife Maura—cold—[43]

Sat. nite O'Connors—Sat. morning was lovely—sunrises & swings & chess—skittles—peaches

Sun.—hangover—love—John's for Scrabble & chess—

I wanted to be w. him tonite too but he wanted to be alone—I need a little time of fasting—to stop smoking to think a lot—

It's a change time—& I need a long session in here—Love & art & me aren't incompatible.

I love him more than I thought—I think loving him this much makes it harder to be alone (sometimes) than it was before I met him—But it's worth it—

UE uptown Tues.—UGH—

I think I'd like to live w. him—I like to be able to look at him all the time—am I just being silly.

43 This is probably Jim Carroll's brother.

Fri. 8:40 Dec. 10

I was right about change—thoughts & feelings are dif. abt. 2 things—Time & JIM & Love

I don't have all the time—I'm not working—true—I'm working 1/2 full time & there's the dentist—so it's practically like a full-time job—so I've got to put a little more value on my time.

That is short, the next isn't—

How have my feelings towards J changed?...I don't feel soft & fuzzy & helpless abt. him—nor are those feelings crawling into other parts of my life...maybe it's a reversal—a self-defense reversal...bec. I've been letting it be obv. that I'll spend as much time w. him as possible...last Sun. he said no...I would have arranged something for tonite...& I guess I'm pissed off (what a bitch) that he's been the one to say no...I'm pissed off at the sit. whc. makes me so pliable... The love haze is gone...bec. of pride?...or am I really being gently rebuffed?...I do want a Wuthering Heights love—total—yet can I do anything else then?—I didn't—now it seems gone & I'll never know—will it come back? I feel we've taken a step away fr. each other...I feel he did it first...w. Sun. & tonite...yet maybe I'm being really silly...I'm dead tonite & really glad to be relaxing here...Sun. we were tired too...maybe I just have too much, but def. more than he a tendency to wring things dry—to revel in the intensest feelings...tonite I'll feel so tamely abt. him (bec. I'm tired?) I feel all statements are shaky...I can't forget what B said abt. statements & trying to understand your life...But Don Juan says clarity is an enemy...

The last week I feel a strong feeling of being myself...I feel tough... OK...prob bec. I'm working...Also I'm less afraid of doing something to wreck Jim & me...but I wonder if being so cocksure means I care less...

Is that mushy togethery feeling just a way to not feel alone & self-determined (as much as we are)—to fool oneself into thinking you're not alone?...& really not esp. connected to the other person? How do I feel abt. Jim tonite? I don't know...I cert. would hate to not see him...but I don't feel all wrapped up in him...to say I love him ...I love lots of people...I still prefer him but the dif. is less...

Then there's that I always feel more for him when I see him...& less & less as I see him less & less...

Think abt. all this—

Appendix

Books and authors Rosemary Mayer read (or aspired to read) and movies and directors she watched in 1971

Listed in the order in which she mentions them in the journal

Gimme Shelter, dir. Albert and David Maysles and Charlotte Zwernin, 1970

Bed and Board, dir. François Truffaut, 1970

Silence: Lectures and Writings, John Cage, 1961

Space, Time and Architecture, Sigfried Giedion, 1941

The Future of Architecture, Frank Lloyd Wright, 1970

A Year from Monday: New Lectures and Writings, John Cage, 1967

To Catch a Thief, dir. Alfred Hitchcock, 1955

The Quiller Memorandum, dir. Michael Anderson, 1966

Roger Corman, dir.

Jack Burnham

Colin Cherry

Claude Lévi-Strauss

Robert Ardrey, possibly *The Territorial Imperative,* 1966

Onibaba, dir. Kaneto Shindo, 1964

The Grapes of Wrath, dir. John Ford, 1940

The Deadly Companions, dir. Sam Peckinpah, 1961

The Diary of Anaïs Nin, possibly Volume 3: 1939-1944, which was published in 1971

Sylvia Plath

Escape from the Planet of the Apes, dir. Don Taylor, 1971

The Complete Illustrated Book of Yoga, Swami Vishnudevananda, 1960

"Russian Psychic Research Book," possibly *Psychic Discoveries Behind the Iron Curtain,* Sheila Ostrander and Lyn Schroeder, 1970

Heraclitus

Henry David Thoreau

The Raw and the Cooked, Claude Lévi-Strauss, 1964

The Teachings of Don Juan: A Yagui Way of Knowledge,
Carlos Castaneda, 1968

The Soft Skin, dir. François Truffaut, 1964

The Seven Minutes, dir. Russ Meyer, 1971

Account Unsettled, Simenon (edition unclear)

Frank Herbert

Back, Henry Green, 1946

The Four-Gated City, Doris Lessing, 1969

The Beguiled, dir. Don Siegel, 1971

A Separate Reality: Further Conversations with Don Juan, Carlos Castaneda, 1971

Lost Horizon, dir. Frank Capra, 1937

The Conformist, dir. Bernardo Bertolucci, 1970

"SF," possibly science fiction

Joan Didion

Self-Revealment: A Memoir, Raphael Soyer, 1969

Ray Bradbury

Brothers Karamazov, dir. Richard Brooks, 1958

Socrates, dir. Roberto Rossellini, 1971

Rosemary Mayer (1943–2014) was a prolific artist involved in the New York art scene beginning in the late 1960s. Best known for her large-scale sculptures using fabric as the primary material, she also created works on paper, artist books, and outdoor installations, all of which explored themes of temporality, history, and biography. She was also a writer, art critic, and translator.

A pioneer of the feminist art movement, she was a founding member of A.I.R. Gallery, the first cooperative gallery for women in the United States, and she had one of the earliest shows there. During the 1970s and 1980s, her work was also shown at many New York City alternative art spaces, including The Clocktower, Sculpture Center, and Franklin Furnace, as well as in university galleries throughout the country. In 1982, *Pontormo's Diary,* her translation of the diary of Mannerist artist Jacopo da Pontormo, was published along with a catalogue of her work.

In 2016, SOUTHFIRST Gallery in Brooklyn exhibited a selection of Mayer's work from the late 1960s and early 1970s. The first major exhibit of her work in over thirty years, it was reviewed in the *New York Times, Art in America, The New Yorker,* and artforum.com. A version of this show was presented at the Lamar Dodd School of Art, University of Georgia, in 2017. *Beware of All Definitions,* a catalogue published in conjunction with this show, was the first major publication on Mayer's work since the 1980s. Her work has also been shown in several recent group exhibitions at Nicelle Beauchene Gallery, Murray Guy, and Bridget Donahue, among other venues. In 2018, Soberscove Press published *Temporary Monuments: Work by Rosemary Mayer, 1977–1982,* a compilation of documentation of Mayer's ephemeral installations.

More information about Rosemary Mayer can be found at www.rosemarymayer.com.